PRAISE FOR
MAKE YOUR CASE

"Even though I am retired after forty-two years before the bar and on the bench, I found myself taking notes as I read Make Your Case. *For all lawyers and other professionals who won or lost but didn't know why, Mr. Rollins explains. This book is a must read for every law student considering a trial practice career."*

Judge W. Eugene Henry
Municipal Court Judge (Ret.)

"As a Fire Captain and Fire Investigator, I have had the opportunity to see Greg carry out the important principles taught in this book for both the prosecution and defense. When someone, like Greg, cares enough about the long term effects for all parties involved, we are all on the win-win side of things."

Rande Ferguson
Fire Captain & Investigator, Palm Springs Fire Department

"Make Your Case *is a wonderfully unique book in that it provides a litigator's vision into the skills and analytical tools that can be used in everyday life. Greg does an excellent job in helping the reader envision the problem at hand, understand the rules that may govern said problem, and apply those rules appropriately to the situation. This is the perfect book for any person in any industry that is looking for the skills to solve problems more effectively, and to increase their positive outcomes both personally and professionally."*

Scott Heist, MSTIM
Expert Legal Technologist & Consultant

"As an attorney and owner of a law practice for over fifteen years, I really enjoyed reading Greg's insights and stories. The principles set forth in his book are useful, not only in legal settings, but in everyday life."

Brent A. Duque
Attorney & Founder, Duque Law Firm

"This book is the real deal. As an entrepreneur, coach, speaker, and someone who has built massive organizations, this book really opened my eyes and gave me a new perspective on success and winning."

Jamil Frazier
Author, CEO, & Founder, Think Life is Different

"As the founder of an at-risk youth program, I know how critical it is to have positive information and books to inspire others, especially taken from real life experiences. There can never be enough. In this book, Greg clearly explains the concepts of how to win and how to overcome."

Mario Dorado
Detective & Youth Community Leader

"Greg's realistic, educational journey has inspired me in my career path as a future public defender. This book opened my eyes to the many tactics used in the courtroom."

Sara Fuso
Law School Student, Tulane University

In Make Your Case, *Greg uses personal stories and history to relate his experience as a trial lawyer directly to the business world. Many of the principles contained in the book are essential to building a successful business. For example, proper preparation is the key to success in both law and business.*

Mark Concannon
Founder & CEO, Concannon Business Consulting

Right thinking, life-changing results

MAKE YOUR CASE

THINK BIG, ACT BOLDLY,
AND WIN ARGUMENTS LIKE
A TOP TRIAL LAWYER

GREG ROLLINS

MAKE YOUR CASE

Copyright © 2021 Greg Rollins

ISBN: 978-1-955362-04-7

Although both the publisher and the author have used reasonable care in preparing this book, the information it contains is distributed "as is" and without warranties of any kind. This book is not intended as legal, financial, or health advice; and not all of the recommendations will be suitable for your situation. Neither the publisher nor the author shall be liable for any costs, expenses, or damages resulting from the use of or reliance on the information contained in this book. The information provided within this book is for general informational and educational purposes only. The author makes no representations or warranties, express or implied, about the completeness, accuracy, reliability, suitability or availability with respect to the information, products, services, or related graphics contained in this book for any purpose. Any use of this information is at your own risk.

The case examples provided in this book are loosely based on actual cases handled during the course of the author's career as a trial lawyer. These case examples are offered to illustrate key concepts only. The facts of these cases have been altered and/or combined with other cases to better illustrate key points and protect the privacy of those involved. All facts on which the original cases are based are considered public information.

Published by
STORY ⅼⅼ CHORUS

*This book is dedicated to my family.
Your love and support are a blessing for
which words alone cannot express my gratitude.
Thank you for everything.*

CONTENTS

CHAPTER 1: BUILDING — 1

CHAPTER 2: EVALUATING — 21

CHAPTER 3: CRITICAL THINKING — 39

CHAPTER 4: PREPARING — 63

CHAPTER 5: UNDERSTANDING — 81

CHAPTER 6: PERSUADING — 99

CHAPTER 7: NEGOTIATING — 115

CHAPTER 8: WINNING AND LOSING — 133

CONCLUSION — 157

ACKNOWLEDGEMENTS — 159

ABOUT THE AUTHOR — 163

CHAPTER 1:
BUILDING

A thirteen-year-old boy went flying across a school desk inches from me. His body slammed into some books, and they toppled to the floor. A fellow student came at him, all arms and fists, tangling with him and sending both of them towards the ground. Their heads banged into the metal desk legs.

There was no way that wasn't going to leave a mark.

I had just given four years of my life and many thousands of dollars to be here for this moment. All the years invested into reading books and imagining ways to make ancient Egypt, the Founding Fathers, and the Napoleonic Wars come alive, all reduced to refereeing a classroom cage fight. As it turned out, these kids didn't need any help making wars come alive.

"Sit down!" I said.

Fist met skin yet again, and the roar in the classroom grew.

"I said sit down!"

The rest of the class transformed from students into a betting crowd at a UFC cage fight, and I wondered how I'd gotten my career path so wrong.

I loved history. I thought it loved me. Yet here I was, locked in a room with a bunch of little criminals, with hours to go before I was free. This was my first day in a real classroom, and I'd already learned an important lesson: I wasn't cut out to be a teacher.

As an undergrad in college, I was sure I'd like being a history teacher. I didn't get a chance to test that theory until my final year of college, six months before graduation, when I had to do some student teaching to finish my degree.

That fight was actually my first time in a classroom setting. Six hours in a middle school classroom with a bunch of thirteen and fourteen-year-olds. I was trying to teach, and they were fighting.

It's really difficult to find teachable moments in the middle of a fight. And getting them to listen and stay on task, even when they weren't fighting, was impossible. Middle school kids have a way of mocking adults that makes a grown person feel like their life has become a vacuum.

I was never going to be a teacher. Ever.

It seemed like I'd laid the wrong foundation for four years and was committed to building a house that, all of a sudden, I'd rather burn to the ground than see finished. That was unfortunate to discover six months before graduating from college with a history degree. What was I supposed to do with that?

I had planned ahead, thankfully. I like to build some extra doors in every plan just in case I need an escape route. Along with the history degree, I had grabbed a minor in administrative studies. I thought maybe someday, after an illustrious teaching career that did not involve daily combat maneuvers, I'd move into school administration or become a principal. One of the classes I took for that minor was business law.

"You should take the business law class," my mother had told me. "You love to argue. You are good at arguing."

She wasn't wrong, but I wasn't sure how to take that. At least she hadn't said I was mouthy, a common description of me during my teenage years. Because yes, as a teenager, I would argue all the time, any time. There was no moment when an argument couldn't feasibly take place. Want me to do my chores? Give me a good reason. Want me to go upstairs? Justify that request. Want me to be quiet? I have freedom of speech.

"Get out of the car," my father said to me one afternoon after we'd returned home from running errands.

I did not get out of the car.

"Get out of the car!"

I decided to push the limits.

"Make me," I said after evaluating the request a second time.

As I ran into the house with my father hot on my heels, fearful of where this very short argument would end, I was busy learning the difference between a careful argument and a smart-mouthed comeback. Looking back, I appreciate that my dad didn't let my rude behavior go unchecked. I learned that you can argue, but you don't have to be rude about it.

To be fair, my grandfather was cut from the same cloth. Mom used to say he'd argue with a milepost. He didn't care if he got any response back—mileposts aren't prone to talking much—but I cared about the responses I got from arguing. To be specific, I preferred to always be right and to always have the last word. In fact, I was King of the Last Word until I got married and discovered that was a bad idea.

> I LEARNED THAT YOU CAN ARGUE, BUT YOU DON'T HAVE TO BE RUDE ABOUT IT.

Yet Mom was onto something with that business law class. As I sat slumped in my car after an awful day teaching, I had no idea how glad I would be that I had listened to her.

A LAW STUDENT ON A TRAIN, CALCULATING RISK

What I loved about that business law class was learning legal definitions and how they could be applied to different situations with very different outcomes.

For example, in the civil (not criminal) realm, *assault* means you made an attempt to harm a person regardless of whether you did or did not touch them. A person had to know you intended to harm them because experiencing that fear is part of the definition. *Battery*, on the other hand, is the actual harmful or offensive physical touch.

I found myself observing life around me, watching people interact and thinking, "Hey, technically that was battery."

It's a whole other world when you're in the grocery store (or teaching middle school history) and are on the lookout for battery. While I found this new worldview fascinating, I'm sure my siblings did not share my fascination as I got into the habit of informing them of every legal consequence to their actions. I'm thankful for their support even as I was trying to find my direction in life.

To really get us thinking about the similarities and differences of legal definitions, my business law professor would ask us to come up with scenarios which would be battery but not assault. For example, if someone clocked you on the head with a bat from behind, it would be battery but not assault because you didn't see them coming and wouldn't have known they intended to hurt you.

I started seeing how you could approach a single problem from many different legal angles. Negligence! Duty of care! Assumption of risk! Every legal definition intertwined uniquely in a situation. Each circumstance had its facts and there was the law that governed those facts. The job of the attorney was to determine whether the laws had been violated.

We'd had mock arguments in class, and the mental gymnastics that went into those were similar to solving logic puzzles. I loved it. But when the class was over, I tucked it away on the shelf where you put one-off elective courses in pursuit of your "real" degree.

Fresh from the teaching, fistfight debacle, my mother's reminder got me thinking about law. I had a history degree, though. What career path would fit well with that?

Funnily enough, law.

Law goes back a long way. The ancient Romans loved to sue each other just as much as people today do. Lawsuits are even referenced in the Bible.

Law is based on history because cases form historical precedent. There are cases over a hundred years old that we still cite, cases that are still the controlling law on some topics. And in law school, when you're reading cases, you find some that go back to old England since civil law—or tort (personal injury) law—started way back in the 1200s to 1300s. People have been hurting themselves on their neighbor's trampoline and suing them for it for centuries.

Law school isn't cheap, though. I was a college student with a part-time job, looking at expensive schools. What options did I have? The idea of taking out $200,000 in debt didn't sound like a solution to the problem of not wanting to be a history teacher. It just sounded like another big problem.

I decided that if I couldn't find a more realistic approach than massive debt, I'd go with plan C.

Granted, I didn't have a plan C yet.

I prayed about it, and I looked at local law schools. One was pretty good, but I was told I had to take the LSAT. With a good enough score, I could get a full-ride scholarship.

There it was, my plan C. Ace the LSAT, get my tuition covered.

One problem, though: the LSAT is a stupid test.

Any attorney will tell you that. It's a test filled with logic problems that you'll never go back to once you've finished it. You'll use algebra in life, you'll use fractions in life, you may even need high school chemistry in life, but you'll never use the LSAT unless you work at a train depot.

Here's what I mean by that: the LSAT seemed like it was full of train problems.

Train X is leaving a station at 12:15 p.m. going 15 miles per hour, and Train Y is leaving a station going 20 miles per hour. At what point will these two trains catch up? You have a bunch of answers, including one that says "not enough information provided," which, for this example, is correct because they never told you which direction the trains were going.

Two potential law students sat down on a train taking their LSAT. One knew he absolutely didn't want to be a history teacher. The other was solving math problems that had missing variables. Which one was more motivated?

That's pretty much the LSAT.

The principles of logic definitely apply in a career of law, but the way the LSAT approaches them is different from the practice of law. I took some LSAT prep classes to restructure the way I thought about problem-solving.

My final score on the LSAT was two points under the level necessary for the full ride. I thought that was pretty good, and yes, they did offer me the full ride scholarship. But it wasn't a first-class full ride with all the amenities. Instead, it was contingent upon grades.

I had to maintain a high GPA or I'd be paying tuition.

I decided to hedge my bets a bit by going to school part-time and putting all my focus on keeping my grades up. I lived at home and chose not to work. My entire approach was a leap of faith, but I wasn't taking a sloppy risk; instead, it was a calculated risk.

You have to be willing to take calculated risks.

Determine the risk, consider the variables, and make decisions based on what's acceptable within that risk. I had to keep my grades up, so I made decisions that would make that possible. Of course, the school didn't tell me that most people didn't keep very high GPAs, which was some critical information that, had I known, may have affected my risk assessment.

ANYTHING BUT TEACHING OR CRIMINAL LAW

I started law school in 2006, and the next year, the Great Recession hurtled the economy into a downward spiral.

I knew I'd need an internship geared toward the kind of law I wanted to practice once I graduated and entered what looked like a very tight workforce. The legal landscape is expansive, and there are endless bodies of law. Civil, criminal, probate, tax, real estate . . . you could be a general practitioner and cover a little bit of everything, but it's really hard to do that.

> YOU HAVE TO BE WILLING TO TAKE CALCULATED RISKS.

Whichever law I'd end up practicing, I knew one thing for sure: I did not want to do criminal law.

Criminal law was scary. It was crawling with criminals, potential wrongful convictions, and guilty people walking free. I didn't want to see horrifying crime scene photos and deal with emotional families and broken lives. Who wants to have constant exposure to people at their worst, doing horrible things to others? But the economy was bad, and when I discovered an internship near where I lived, one that paid real money for the entire ten weeks, I was inclined to take it no matter what.

It was at the Riverside County District Attorney's Office. It was criminal law. But it paid, and that was rare.

I ended up in the appellate unit, which is where you work with appeals. With criminal trials, you go in front of the judge and argue facts. If that decision is appealed, you go in front of a panel of appellate judges and argue law. You try to show that the trial judge made a mistake in their ruling or that some other legal aspect failed. It has less to do with facts and more to do with how the law was handled. Cases in the appellate system can work all the way up to the US Supreme Court.

Surprisingly, I loved the appellate system with its legal writing. It reminded me of everything I liked about the business law class, and I ended up coming back the next year as an intern. It was during that second year I got the rare chance to argue one of the briefs I'd drafted as a first-year intern in front of the appellate court.

It was an interesting case. A guy had been robbing convenience stores and was sentenced and convicted for robbery. He had over fifteen prior strike convictions. California has a three-strikes law, meaning that your third violent felony sends you away for twenty-five years to life. Judges have some discretion, though, and in this case, the judge tossed out all but one of those prior strike convictions.

Not fifteen strikes. Not even three strikes. Just one. Over fifteen convictions dropped down to one. It was lunacy. However, the judge justified his ruling by saying that since the robberies had occurred in a short three-month time span, they were part of a single course of conduct. The DA's (district attorney's) office, where I was interning, said it was an abuse of the judge's discretion. Because we argue law in the appellate system and not guilt or innocence, we pointed out that the judge had given no reasons on record for why he'd made that sweeping decision.

Arguing that brief sealed the deal for me. The judge was overruled, and from then on, criminal law it was. And who knows, maybe I would end up seeing those fistfighting students again after all.

Of course, arguing that one brief didn't make me an expert. The DA's office had a closing argument tournament with real stakes: the winner would be offered a job. In a terrible economy, that was a serious carrot.

They gave us a set of fact patterns we were supposed to argue, with each intern given a tournament bracket to play off each other.

For my first round, I gave it my best. Unfortunately, my best was horrible. I was low-energy. I was monotone. I put people to sleep.

The supervising DA, with arms crossed, gave me a pretty good closing argument of his own.

"I hated every minute of it."

The intern competing against me must have been phenomenally bad because I moved on to the next round. That night, I practiced and practiced. I listened to the feedback and reworked my approach.

Closing arguments are the sexy part of any trial, you see.

They're the big showpiece, the sales pitch to the jury. You've bored them with witness questions and endless detail for days or weeks, but now you wrap it up with a big bow and sell them on why they should vote guilty or not guilty. It's what people imagine jury trials should be like from watching TV and movies.

I came back the next day for round two and went completely in the other direction.

I was yelling and screaming, rocking back and forth. I knocked it out of the ballpark . . . into the next ballpark, through a plate glass window, through traffic . . . and it kept going. There's nothing like an overcorrection to generate even more feedback.

"You were screaming at me," the supervising DA said. "I was too uncomfortable to even look at you. You were red in the face and completely non-credible. Somehow, today was even worse than yesterday. I'd rather take a nap than be yelled at!"

Needless to say, I was eliminated that round and I got to watch my peers move on.

I wanted a job there. But, because the DA's office prided itself on trials and I lacked experience with anything involving a trial—selecting a jury, examining witnesses—getting hired seemed unlikely. But the calculated risk mindset kicked in, and I decided to put in the work to go after what I wanted.

I signed up for a trial practice class my next semester of law school to learn how to present evidence, how to control my courtroom manner (preferably somewhere between putting everyone to sleep and making them cry in discomfort), and how to speak so people would want to listen.

I knew what success would look like. It would look like getting the job at the DA's office.

THE GOVERNMENT SHOULD NEVER LOSE A CASE

Calculated risks don't always pan out, but I did get the job at the DA's office after law school. I was placed in Indio, a city not far from Palm Springs. Sounds nice, right? A resort town surely has little crime. Probably some jaywalking or stealing beach towels or something?

Every jurisdiction has crime. Types of crime vary, but crime is everywhere, no exceptions. Affluent areas might not get violent drug crimes, but you'll find domestic violence and white-collar crime. As a new prosecutor, I had to get a feel for the place as far as the crimes that happened there, and how the people viewed certain crimes. This would impact jury selection.

It sounds strange, but to different demographics and cultures, some crimes are acceptable. There are a lot of older people in Palm Springs, and their generational culture views some crimes very hard while others are given a pass. For example, remember the show *I Love Lucy* from the 1950s? There are dozens of episodes with situations that make us cringe today but were perfectly acceptable then. Like when Lucy's husband, Ricky, loses his temper and spanks her for bad behavior—yeah, not going to fly today. But this illustrates the generational gap as to what is and is not acceptable, and I needed to consider that in jury selection.

It wasn't long into my career in Indio when I got to see this firsthand. I had a case that everyone said was a slam dunk.

A man was visiting family. A woman unrelated to the family, staying in the house, woke up from a nap to find that man grabbing her crotch. The police got involved and caught the suspect trying to escape. While he admitted to doing it, he tried to explain his way free.

"I meant to touch her shoulder," he told police. "But my hand accidentally moved and I ended up grabbing her crotch."

Since that was ridiculous, he then claimed she had indicated to him that she wanted him to do it . . . even though she'd been asleep. By the end of it, the guy had all but provided me with a confession to work from, and I was feeling confident. The first sign of trouble with this seemingly slam dunk case started with an older judge being assigned to the case.

"Why are you guys even prosecuting this?" he grumped. "Back in my day, this wasn't even a crime. Every red-blooded American male has probably done this."

I was shocked.

The case went to trial. The jury heard various statements. The defendant even testified, and I questioned him thoroughly. There were a bunch of people who watched the trial, including senior attorneys, and they all agreed that I did a great job. They were sure it was going to be a fast conviction.

The jury came back soon, that was true, but with a not guilty verdict. Not a hung jury, not with questions, but full-on *not guilty*.

The dude walked. I was upset. The victim hadn't gotten any justice.

Even though the evidence was there, the jury had chosen not to convict. I learned very early on that just because there's sufficient evidence, doesn't mean the jury will necessarily vote according to what that evidence shows. There's a wide range of other factors that come into play. These can include the likability of the witness or the defendant, the persuasiveness of the attorneys, rulings by the judge, or even mistakes made in the investigation. I learned that just because the law says something is illegal, doesn't mean the jury will always agree.

The jury had no idea about a past assault and how it had affected her. They weren't given that context. They only saw her freaking out over being touched. They saw her testimony on the stand and couldn't understand why she was crying and struggling to talk about the incident. They were completely unsympathetic, and the judge actually thanked them as they were leaving, telling them that they made the right decision.

That was a terrible moment that I am glad happened to me as a lawyer.

I couldn't control the jury. I couldn't control the judge. Things don't always play out like you think they will. That early loss taught me I could lose and there is no such thing as a slam dunk case.

From then on, every time I would get a case, I evaluated its strengths and weaknesses much like I would when assessing calculated risks for difficult decisions. I would imagine the arguments the opponent would make, whether or not I thought they were valid.

THE TRUTH IS, YOU LEARN MORE FROM YOUR LOSSES THAN YOU DO YOUR WINS.

The truth is, you learn more from your losses than you do your wins.

As a prosecutor, I did thirty-nine jury trials and two bench trials (trials without a jury) in just under ten years. Out of twenty-two misdemeanor trials, I got eighteen guilty verdicts. That's a decent number of trials and seems like a great run of wins, but ideally it should have been 100 percent guilty verdicts. The government should get a conviction in every case because, if the system is working correctly, you should only go to trial in cases where the conviction is locked tight. There should be no reasonable doubt.

Still, it seemed like I was having a good run, even winning Misdemeanor Prosecutor of the Year at the DA's office two years in a row. I had a great future as a winning prosecutor. But there are a lot of politics in the DA's office. Yards of red tape. Micromanagement. Politics. More politics. My private life was in a constant state of interruption from last-minute trial assignments.

Even worse, I had this gnawing sense that my view of ethical justice was beginning to differ in some ways from that of the DA's office. This was one of several reasons why I began considering the switch from prosecutor to defense attorney.

To help you understand why, let me tell you about how bail works.

WHAT JUSTICE LOOKS LIKE

Say you're arrested and you go in on $50,000 bail. You pay the $50,000 and you get out of jail. As long as you show up for court, you get your money back whether you're guilty or not. Bail is basically insurance that you'll show up in court.

But if you're like many people, you don't have $50,000 on hand. You don't have friends or family who can help you out, and you don't have property to take a lien on. So, your choice is either to sit in jail until your trial or find another place to get the bail money.

Sitting in jail isn't really an option.

Let's say it's a misdemeanor you were arrested for, and they have thirty days to bring you to trial. During the COVID-19 pandemic, there was little courtroom activity because of emergency orders, so the date of your trial kept getting extended another thirty days, and another thirty days, and another thirty days—you get the idea. Now do felonies, which allow sixty days to bring you to your preliminary hearing and then another sixty days to bring you to trial. Extend those trial dates with that math.

If you don't have bail, you might be sitting in jail a long time. Try keeping your job or home, or taking care of your family, while behind bars, just waiting to have your day in court. So yes, we're all "guaranteed" the right to a speedy trial, but sometimes that doesn't happen in a manner anyone would consider speedy.

So what you do is, you go to a bail bond company and ask them to post bail for you. They happily do so but there's a catch.

"We'll pay the $50,000, but we'll need 10 percent," they might tell you, meaning you have to pay them $5,000 outright, nonrefundable. Whether you're found guilty or not guilty, go to court every day like a good citizen, or have your case dismissed, you'll never see your $5,000 again.

Situations like these are tough for people—especially for folks who turn out to be innocent and may already struggle to make ends meet. The more times I watched peoples' lives get upended in these kinds of bureaucratic scenarios, the more I felt pulled in a different direction.

Don't get me wrong, I loved being a prosecutor. I loved seeking justice for crime victims. I loved the feeling of contributing to my community's safety. But there were some aspects of the job I did not like. Working for the District Attorney's Office came with layers of rules, regulations, policy, and politics. Overall, the District Attorney's Office was filled with prosecutors who were on a similar mission as me: to seek justice. However, what that justice looks like differs from person to person.

When it comes to serious things, people tend to have a similar sense of justice, but when you get into less serious stuff, opinions differ. For example, some believe that it's unjust to drive even one-mile per hour over the posted speed limit (for any reason). I know firsthand, because my grandmother is a prime example! Then there are the people who view the speed limit as more of a guideline than a hard-and-fast rule. As long as they don't drive faster than five-miles per hour over the speed limit, everything's fine in their mind. Interestingly enough, my grandfather falls into this category. (You can imagine the conversations had in their vehicle depending on who was driving!)

So, if my grandfather were to get a speeding ticket for driving three-miles per hour over the speed limit, he would feel like he was being treated unjustly. My grandmother, though, would feel like justice was being served because he was indeed speeding—and she would also be there to give a well-earned *I told you so* eye-roll.

For me, while I agreed with the mission of the District Attorney's Office, my own personal sense of justice was leading me in a new direction. Throughout the course of my career, I had learned that there are always two sides to every story.

1. DEFINE YOUR SUCCESS

Big changes generally start much earlier than the moment you make the leap. For each case I tried, I learned to define what success would look like. Maybe I didn't care if all the charges came back guilty, for example, as long as a specific charge did. The point is, when it comes to success, *you* have to define it, not someone else. What *you* think success looks like is unique to you.

Success is tied to your goal, and that isn't always what will make the most money. I had to look at success from every angle. For me, stress, family, and ethical concerns were angles I had to consider as part of the picture of success.

Leaving the DA's office to go out on my own was risky, but knowing what initial success would look like—I didn't have to be Johnnie Cochran in six months, for example—allowed me to take the initial steps.

Without knowing how you define success, you can't calculate risk. If you can't calculate risk, you won't take a step.

2. DO THE WORK

You never get from point A to point B if you don't do anything.

Once I decided to become a defense attorney, I started doing the work. I leveraged my network for recommendations and advice. For example, I used a web designer recommended by someone in my network to create my new website. Other connections provided industry advice, such as the need for a new wardrobe or what to prepare for as a defense attorney. Using my network connections meant I didn't have to reinvent the wheel. The people I'd surrounded myself with were a great resource and made doing the work that much easier.

All your work should be toward the success goal you defined. Find solutions to the problems that get in front of you. They don't go away without work.

3. MAKE YOUR MOVE

Making your move is all about timing, and that requires self-discipline and self-restraint.

During a domestic abuse case I tried as a prosecutor, I had the defendant on the stand and a series of questions I planned to ask him. He refused to acknowledge he'd beat up his wife, so I tried a different approach and asked him if he was an angry person.

"Well yeah, sometimes I get upset," he said.

"Let me take you back. You're the only breadwinner for the family," I said.

"Yeah."

"You work long, hard nights."

"Yeah, that's right."

"You should be respected."

"Yeah, that's right!"

"In your opinion, she hasn't contributed much," I said.

"No, she's lazy! She doesn't even do the dishes."

"And she nags you a lot."

"All the time!"

"And so, on this day we're talking about, she was nagging you again."

"Yeah!"

"That probably annoyed you, or made you a little angry, because she was so disrespectful. You were entitled to be a little angry."

"Yeah! She deserved what she got!"

And that was the opening I needed.

I could have gone on with my planned questions, or I could take that opening and drop the hammer to show the jury that, up until now, the defendant had said nothing happened—and here he was, saying she deserved what she got.

If my timing is off, I interrupt and lose the flow of what's happening, and I close the perfect opening. I have to pay attention and not lock myself into the questions I planned on asking, being willing to let the witness use their own words to give me an opening. Sometimes what I am expecting isn't where the witness takes me, and suddenly I'm given an opportunity I hadn't planned for.

About three weeks before the COVID-19 pandemic caused the country to shut down, word got around the DA's office that I was thinking of leaving. Word getting out sped up the timeline I'd planned for, and I left shortly thereafter.

Had I followed my plan and waited just a few weeks longer to quit, there would have been no way I could have left. You don't quit a job in the middle of an economy-crushing pandemic when getting back to normal pre-pandemic life isn't even on the horizon.

> YOU CAN'T DROP THE HAMMER IF YOU HAVEN'T EVEN PICKED IT UP.

Like questioning the witness, I could've stuck to my plan, or taken the opening that presented itself. I went for the opening and wasn't worried, because I'd made a plan that helped me get the work done. Without both, you can't make your move even if the timing is perfect. You can't drop the hammer if you haven't even picked it up.

The moment I saw those middle schoolers sail through the air in the middle of my lecture, I knew my life was going to drastically change. I've made a lot of decisions since then that seemed risky, but you make or break your success by your ability to evaluate what's going on, what it means, and determining the action you'll take.

IF YOU BUILD IT...

Sure, I made some big moves. But it's important to see that I'd laid a foundation sturdy enough to build a law practice on. While I didn't have every detail under control, I'd put in the work. As a history major, I'd studied and honed my ability to research. As an intern, I had learned to evaluate cases and craft arguments. As a prosecutor, I had learned how to exhaustively prepare for cases. As a defense attorney, I've become a master persuader and negotiator.

The rest of this book is filled with these lessons and more. But the most important step to launching any new venture—be it a career path, a business, or anything else—is laying a strong foundation. No foundation, no house.

THE STRUCTURE YOU WANT TO BUILD IN YOUR LIFE DETERMINES THE FOUNDATION THAT YOU NEED TO LAY.

A foundation is crucial to everything in life, from the questions asked in every trial to the way we structure our lives.

In a trial, the foundation I've built leading up to it limits the kinds of questions I'm allowed to ask on how evidence can be introduced.

The structure you want to build in your life determines the foundation that you need to lay. Do you need a reputation for excellence? Do you need a brand associated with winning? Do you need to develop a diverse network of well-connected leaders? Do you need to build skills you don't have right now? Your foundation is really the answer to this simple question: what does my definition of success require?

You might remember the popular movie *Field of Dreams*. Kevin Costner plays baseball fanatic Ray Kinsella. One evening, while walking through his cornfield, a voice whispers, "If you build it, he will come." In the movie, this is all about building a baseball diamond and reconciling with his father. In your life, though, building a foundation will mean attracting opportunities. I don't promise there will be thousands of them magically knocking at your door. However, you will have many opportunities in life and business.

The real catch becomes which ones you should take and which ones you should pass on. Just like the cases a lawyer takes on or declines define their career, the opportunities you pursue or pass over will define yours. So how do you know when to say yes, no, or maybe?

Now that you've built your foundation, how to evaluate opportunities like a lawyer is exactly what we're going to talk about next.

CLOSING REMARKS

Every goal is set on a foundation.

Your success in reaching that goal depends on how well you've built your foundation. What you build at the start determines what you'll end up with.

To build a solid foundation, I have a methodical approach I've used time and time again:

1. Define what success looks like to you for this specific goal.
2. Do the hard work in pursuit of your goal.
3. Make your move when the timing is right.

Making a habit of this process will help you succeed in setting and reaching new goals in the future.

You might have big goals, but what kind of foundation are you building? Does it allow you to alter direction and make decisions as situations change around you? Is it a foundation that promotes personal growth, or does it force you to stand still?

Dreams don't materialize without a concrete foundation.

CHAPTER 2:
EVALUATING

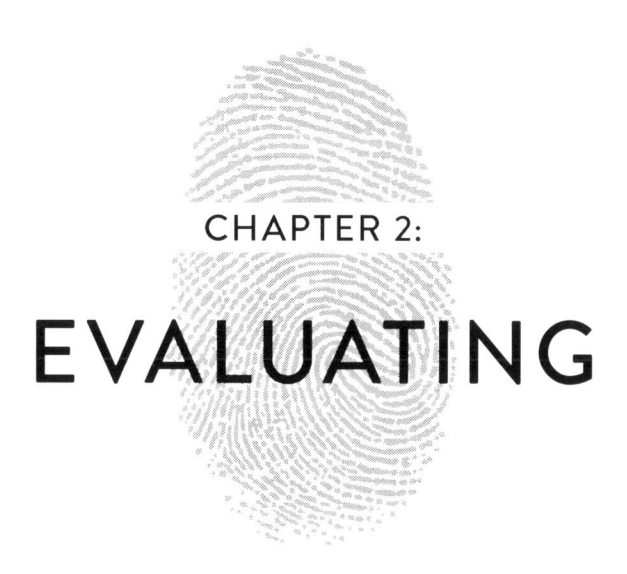

There are a lot of ways to kill a person.

It was Friday night at a local cowboy bar. The music was loud, and people were on their way to the bottom of the bottle, some line dancing in their boots while others flowed from the bar to the parking lot and back again. Petty romantic arguments, the kind that came after a few drinks, could be heard mixed in with the music.

A small group of people had gathered near the entrance of the bar. The chatter grew heated, but most people paid no attention until they saw the shadow of a woman go flying through the air. Within seconds, a body crashed into the rough wooden barn door that was propped open, sending bits of glass and wood in every direction. A decorative wooden railing snapped, with sharp fragments of lumber jutting up from the ground. Cowboys were rolling around like tumbleweeds.

For a moment, people froze. And then the 911 call center lit up.

"My friend was just stabbed!" said a frantic caller. The operator tried to calm the caller down as police were dispatched to the scene.

When they arrived, they found an angry group of people in chaos, loud honky-tonk music still blaring from inside the bar.

"She just came at me with a knife," the victim said, holding her hand to her neck, her arms and face crisscrossed with cuts. "I have no idea why! I was just standing here, minding my own business, and she attacked me." She dramatically told of how my client had threatened her and eventually attacked her using a knife she pulled out of her purse. She described it as some kind of flip knife with a black handle. The detail she shared was remarkable for such a chaotic scene.

Yet, even as the victim described to the police what had happened, she refused medical attention. I've seen cases where someone was seriously beat up, where they'd been purposefully attacked with a weapon. They'd had teeth knocked out, broken noses heading sideways, and blood gushing from cracked foreheads. They definitely hadn't turned down a trip in the ambulance.

It seemed pretty bad for the accused, my client. Eyewitnesses told police my client was there, and it was no secret that she was dating the victim's ex-boyfriend. Attacking someone with a knife deserves serious justice, like years in prison, right? That was exactly what my client was looking at.

Yet, something about the whole case seemed off to me. For one thing, the victim wasn't dead.

You get a knife to the neck, as she'd described, and you'd probably be dead. And if you were miraculously alive, you definitely don't refuse medical care, because you should be bleeding out all over the place. Most stabbing victims didn't hang around to provide an elaborate statement to the police while refusing medical care.

I evaluated the details of the case, including what my client said had really happened.

The victim shows up at the bar. She sees her ex-boyfriend with his new girlfriend, my client, standing outside near the entrance. She decides to do a little trash-talking because it wouldn't be a Friday night at the bar if you didn't do that. Then she goes in, gets herself a drink, and goes back to pick up where she left off. Things get uglier, the volume gets loud enough to top the music from inside, and people start getting in each other's faces.

It was when the shoving started that the real damage got underway. Tempers got heated, my client's boyfriend got in between them, and the next thing you know, he's tossing his ex-girlfriend through the wooden door. Large chunks and splinters of wood from the door went everywhere. Nicks and cuts filled with blood. There was a lot of screaming. People called 911.

As soon as I looked at the pictures from the crime, I had a strong feeling that something was seriously off with the case.

EVALUATION DETERMINES YOUR BEHAVIOR

When this case came to me and I considered taking on the client, I had three basic areas in which I evaluated it.

First, as a lawyer, I needed to evaluate whether there was a real opportunity for a good outcome with the best defense I could provide based on the evidence. I had to consider how I would be able to help the person.

Second, as a business owner, I needed to evaluate how much time and effort it would take to try the case. This area is about the scope and the bandwidth, a question of how much time it will take to handle the case.

Third, I needed to evaluate it based on my personal morals and ethics. I've set some rules for myself regarding which cases I'll take on. We'll talk about this a bit later.

I took the stabbing case because I could see, after evaluating the evidence and facts of the case, that there was the potential of a very good defense for my client.

But first, I needed an investigator to do some digging.

When I worked in the DA's office, we had easy access to investigators. These were people who were true law enforcement, whose job it was to work as investigators for the prosecutor. We'd send them out for additional information, which could mean anything from stakeouts to serving subpoenas.

While I still had connections with some of the investigators I'd worked with, I was a defense attorney now. I had to pay for them out of pocket.

The photos from the crime scene were crying out for more investigation, though, so I contacted a surgeon at a nearby hospital who had served in the army as a combat doctor. I brought him up to speed on the basics of the case, including the alleged victim's claims of being stabbed.

"I'd like to send you some evidence photos," I said. "Would you be willing to take a look at them and give me your expert opinion? I'd like to know what you think about the injuries you see in the images."

As a combat doctor, he had experience with lots of different kinds of wounds, and he said he was willing to review the evidence. I sent over the photos of the injuries and waited. When he got back to me, he defined the injuries as bruises and cuts.

"There's nothing in these photos that would be a knife or stabbing wound," he said. "It looks more like what I'd see in a fight or accident. You get stabbed or slashed in the neck like the victim described, you're dead, and there's blood everywhere."

He went on to describe the scenario, down to the last detail of blood splatter and what happens when a knife is pulled out, reenacting it as the victim described it in her statements to the police.

"When the knife is pulled out of that kind of wound, blood is everywhere. It's on you, the knife, the victim . . . and if you're slashing at a person, there's blood spatter on everyone and everything around. The complete lack of blood splatter in the photos doesn't match what she says happened. And again, she's not dead." He pointed out the broken door and the glass from the window and bottles. "I'll tell you how these injuries occurred. This broken door is what scraped her neck and face. Those photos don't look like any knife wound I've ever seen. A knife makes a clean slice. These are jagged and rough."

I'd already done an interview with my client that backed up the doctor's assessment. After reviewing the evidence again, I was sure he was correct. Based on that, I knew the DA might have difficulty proving the assault with a knife charge. I quickly filed a motion to get the doctor qualified as an expert so he could testify.

I was starting to feel pretty confident about the case when a friend of my client called my office and offered to testify that my client wasn't even there that night.

"I could say she wasn't at the bar," the friend said. "I would be willing to say it was someone else, maybe someone who looked a bit like her, like a twin sister."

That was a terrible idea.

"Does she have a twin sister?" I asked.

"No," the friend said. "But she didn't do what that woman is accusing her of. She's just out to get my friend for dating her ex. Wouldn't it be better to just say she wasn't there?"

"Absolutely not—that's a horrible idea! Other people saw her there," I told her. We were looking for the best defense, not the worst defense imaginable. Pretending she had a twin sister was right out of a soap opera. "She's already told the police she was there. If you change the story at trial to something obviously false, the jury isn't going to look too kindly on that."

There's nothing like completely destroying your credibility in front of the jury and making them think your whole case is dubious by having a witness appear out of nowhere and make claims that the prosecution could easily disprove. It would make both my client and me look bad. Her best defense was one based on the truth, not on what someone else wanted the truth to be.

A FALSE REALITY IS NEVER CREDIBLE

Never lie. Never try to create a false reality. Everything has to be stacked up against the truth.

You have to look for reasonable conclusions that are based on what is true. It doesn't matter if you're a prosecutor, a defense attorney, or an average citizen faced with daily decisions. You have to evaluate whether what you're told makes sense and if it fits with the facts you have.

The best defense is one supported by evidence because that's a *credible* defense.

Best defense = credible defense. Remember that.

As a defense attorney, I have an arsenal of potential defenses, but the key is to find the best one for each case. Is it a credible alibi? A missing element to establish the crime? A motive to fabricate the crime? A legal nuance? A lack of credible prosecution evidence? Another option is to concede things that are true but not incriminating, which builds credibility. Sometimes the best defense is just to be the most credible lawyer in the room.

> SOMETIMES THE BEST DEFENSE IS JUST TO BE THE MOST CREDIBLE LAWYER IN THE ROOM.

In this case, as in every case, the DA had to prove every single element on every single charge, but as a defense attorney, I only had to prove *a* defense. Not every possible defense, just the *best* one.

My client would probably have loved to say she wasn't at the bar that night or have someone testify to that effect for her. But being present at the bar wasn't a crime. It was true but not incriminating. Being present didn't prove my client stabbed the victim or even threatened to do so.

This was about the question of reasonable doubt.

In California, the law that is read to the jury in a criminal case comes from the Judicial Council of California Criminal Jury Instructions, the CALCRIM. It's basically 2,500 pages of jury instructions, listing every element that could come up for a case. As an attorney, I submit a list of CALCRIM jury instructions that I want the judge to read based on how I'm approaching the case. This is to help the jury know what qualifies as evidence and what would be considered beyond reasonable doubt.

The prosecution has the burden to prove their case beyond reasonable doubt. The victim's story was clearly sketchy based on the evidence and what both my client and the investigator had told me. So I started taking a look at the victim herself as a possible defense against the alleged intimidation. If I could show the jury where the gaps were in the victim's story, they wouldn't believe she was credible.

As it turns out, I didn't have to look far for those gaps.

The DA offered my client a significantly reduced sentence, not even factoring in prior criminal history, if the client pled guilty to a lesser charge. When the DA extends you a lowball offer, you have to ask why. Did the DA miss something? Did I miss something? Does the DA think the case is weak? I suspected it was the last one, that the DA didn't have a strong case. I simply had to get a little momentum in that direction, and I found it in the alleged victim's criminal history.

Serious felonies. Pending convictions for a violent assault. This woman was no angel. Perhaps she was hoping to hand over my client in return for a lighter sentence of her own, hoping she could make a deal somewhere down the line.

I sent the investigator out to find witnesses to some of those previous cases. If we added their testimonies to her violent criminal history and her questionable story of what happened, then the victim would be seen in a new light.

"We have all kinds of reasons to distrust the alleged victim. The evidence, her history, her motive to lie," I could say. "And all these things lead to the same conclusion, that this woman is not a credible witness. If the prosecution's star witness is not credible, then chances are the charges are not credible. That's reasonable doubt."

These are things I could bring up to the jury. They could evaluate it on their own.

Remember, everyone is innocent unless proven guilty. *Beyond a reasonable doubt* is the evaluation process the jury has to use to get there.

EVALUATION IS KEY

Evaluation is the bedrock of knowing when to say yes.

Yes, I'll take the case.

Yes, he's guilty.

Yes, I believe her.

Yes, I'll invest in your company.

Yes, I'll marry you.

Every decision we make comes after some kind of evaluation we make. Not everyone has a great evaluation process, however. If you don't have a correct read on the situation—if you can't see it in context—you have virtually no chance of making the right decisions. Your ability to look at surrounding circumstances and pull out the details to make a judgment call is what will make or break your success.

It's like poker. If you think you have a good hand, you bet more money. But if you think your hand isn't great, you either fold or you bluff. The whole time you're playing, you're evaluating the probability of winning. You're weighing the strength of your own hand and trying to figure out whether what the other players have in their hands will beat you.

But you're not only evaluating the cards, you're also evaluating the other players, looking for patterns. Do they seem nervous? How have they been playing the game? Does that guy seem to be sweating an awful lot right now? If you evaluate correctly, you can spot a bluff or when another player just got the card he needed and you should get out of the game.

At the same time, you have to keep your poker face. You must be conscious of presenting yourself in the way you want to be evaluated, probably with confidence and strength. You're framing how you want the rest of the players to view you.

THE PROCESS OF SMART EVALUATION

Evaluation can be summed up in one question: should I?

It's a question that kick-starts the thought process of evaluation. You can't start thinking about what your next move ought to be if you never ask yourself, "Should I?" Without that question, there is no next move.

Imagine you're out on a beautiful lake. It's frozen. There are some ice houses closer to shore. Bright sun, light breeze, mild temperatures. It seems like a good place to be, until you hear a loud cracking sound.

Was it the ice cracking? Was it some irate ice fisherman taking an illegal potshot at a fish through a hole in the ice? Whatever it was, your first question is, "Should I get off of this ice?" Yeah, you really should. But smart evaluation helps you decide which way to go. After all, what if you start running toward shore, but that's where the cracks are forming? Not good, unless you like cold baths.

Your "should I?" question isn't as simple as whether or not to bolt off the ice; it's also about evaluating how to do it safely.

DOES THIS SUPPORT MY WHY?

Everything I do as a defense attorney has to fit with why I left the prosecutor's office. I had specific goals in mind; why would I say yes to something that didn't fit those goals?

I left because I wanted to help people, of course, but I had personal motivations for leaving too. Missing out on family moments because of last-minute case assignments and eighty-hour work weeks was something I wanted in my rearview mirror. There's no way I'd want to turn the car around and go back to that. Plus, I wanted autonomy in choosing cases. If yes is my default answer, the cases are choosing me.

Every case I take on as a defense attorney has to support the reasons why I left the DA's office.

The first rule of evaluation goes back to chapter 1, the goals you set. You'll need them when it comes to evaluating. If the decision you're about to make goes against those goals, it doesn't support your *why*.

AM I AN EXPERT?

Considering your expertise as a part of your evaluation isn't so much about being a know-it-all as it is a question of time.

Arrested for possession of illegal drugs? Intent to sell? Domestic violence? Assault? These are all cases I could do with my eyes closed because I've done so many of them.

"Well, Greg, I didn't assault anyone, but I did embezzle money from the county fund. Clearly it's not as violent as assaulting someone. Will you take my case?"

Early on, before I had much experience with those types of cases, I'd have said no.

An embezzlement case like that is what's known as a paper case, and I wasn't an expert. I'd be facing stacks of banker's boxes full of reports and records that I'd have to go through. If I said yes to a paper case, I could find myself going through thousands of documents for endless hours, matching transactions and verifying line by line. And I'd have to do that for each count of embezzlement.

> EVERY CASE I TAKE ON AS A DEFENSE ATTORNEY HAS TO SUPPORT THE REASONS WHY I LEFT THE DA'S OFFICE.

Not only would that take a significant amount of time just to get through all the records, but I'd have to get up to speed on that area of law and how to try the case.

If I'm going to spend that much time on a case, knowing it's not it's not my area of expertise and it will require a serious investment of time, I have two ways to answer that potential client. It could be yes, but the cost of representation has to be higher. Or it might simply be a strong no.

IS IT WORTH IT?

"Greg, I got a traffic ticket I need your help with."

So far, so good.

"I'm in Blythe."

No thanks.

Because Blythe, though still in my county, is near the Arizona border. The cost of driving there, taking up at least an entire day for a low financial return, is not worth it.

This is about opportunity cost. Every opportunity that comes your way has a cost. What will it cost me financially? What will it cost my reputation? What will it cost in time? What is the cost to my family? All decisions have a value on them once you start to understand opportunity cost. When you're evaluating, you should always be counting the cost.

When I first started out as a defense attorney, my wife and I agreed that I would chase any possible paid case. It didn't take long to revisit that decision, because I ended up taking cases I regretted. Since I was new to choosing my own cases, it was often a gut feeling, not experience or measuring the distance from home to Blythe, that told me to avoid a client.

"I'm being charged with shoplifting," a man said on the phone.

The case seemed easy enough. The man said he had truly forgotten to pay for an item in his cart and now, facing the potential for an embarrassing shoplifting charge, he was freaking out. In fact, he seemed to be freaking out a little too much. He was acting like this potential shoplifting charge could put him behind bars for the rest of his life.

I felt uneasy, even as I found myself explaining over the phone how I'd take the case and offering a reduced rate if no charges were filed.

It should have been worth it from the surface. Nothing about the case itself was challenging. But as the weeks went by, my phone kept ringing. First once a week, then twice. Evenings were spent consoling and comforting the client, reassuring him that there was no conspiracy against him. I began to dread the sound of the phone ringing.

High stress, low money, definitely not worth it. I should have listened to my gut and never taken the case. But I didn't.

And I let another case choose me.

A man in his mid-forties called me one day, upset about what was happening with his twenty-two-year-old son, who had been accused of assaulting his cousin. Would I represent the young man?

I had a gut feeling that something was off, but it seemed straightforward enough, and I agreed to take the case.

And then, for what seemed like endless weeks, my client continued to call. Calls at night. Calls on the weekend. Calls over the holidays. Calls to go visit the son in jail. Calls wanting case updates. Calls in a panic.

Pretty soon, I realized what I'd gotten myself into. This family had a history of court cases with ex-wives and old girlfriends. The young cousin who was accusing the man's son had a habit of going on social media and making all kinds of wild claims. On top of that, the twenty-two-year-old son was way too calm for being a first-timer in jail. It should have been clear to me that this wasn't his first rodeo.

I should have quickly seen that things weren't conforming to my understanding of the facts. I should have trusted my initial instincts.

I needed to ask myself, "who has the control in this situation?"

I do. And if my default is no, something has to legitimately tip the scales toward yes.

Now when someone calls, I try to get a feel for the person and the situation. Some of that comes with experience in dealing with people and getting a sense for how certain people respond in situations. You build an instinct for reading people and patterns of behavior.

Remember the poker game. You're evaluating people as much as the cards.

IS THIS WINNABLE?

I'm an attorney. I want to win. I'm pretty sure my clients want me to win too.

But I'm not going to get a client's hopes up when I can tell the case is an uphill battle and they aren't going to get everything they want. Anyone can take your money and promise a dismissal, but I'd rather paint a picture of reality.

Winning takes on many forms as long as you're honest at the start. My job is not to tell you what you want to hear and then cash your check. It's

WINNING TAKES ON MANY FORMS AS LONG AS YOU'RE HONEST AT THE START.

to evaluate whether the details of the case fit with reality and if there's even a legitimate path to getting what you want. I tell my clients, "I may not always tell you what you want to hear, but I will always tell you what you need to hear."

"Look, you're facing ten years, and I think you're going to get your ass kicked in trial," I might tell you if you were a client with a messy case. You can still ask me to proceed anyway, or you can take my advice and settle for a lesser sentence. But at least your whole family isn't assuming you'll get off unscathed and are shocked when you get sent away for a decade.

This isn't just about treating clients with respect; it's also good business. If I string someone along with false hope and promises all the way to state prison, not only did I hurt them, but they're not going to refer me to family and friends. I'm not going to get good reviews online. I'm going to hurt my reputation. And more importantly, I'm not going to be maintaining what I've built.

IS IT MORAL?

You have to have ethical guidelines and know where you draw the line because, sooner or later, decisions will crash up against it.

There are certain cases I don't want to touch. It isn't so much a question of not wanting to help a person, but having an understanding of the larger picture.

Imagine getting a phone call from a woman calmly telling you her nephew has been arrested for having twenty pounds of meth in his car. And, oh yeah, she's willing to pay top dollar for representation. All up front and in cash.

"They found the meth during a routine traffic stop," she says. "Will you take the case?"

Her complete calm and willingness to pay cash up front let me know the traffic stop isn't the only fishy thing about this case.

Of all the times you've been pulled over by the police, how many times did they find twenty pounds of meth in the trunk of your car? How many times did they even search and find the fast food bags on the floor of the back seat? How many times have you been pulled over by a K-9 unit?

I don't know what the probability is, but there are some arrests that aren't lucky breaks for the police. If you're pulled over for a traffic stop by a K-9 unit, something's up. There's some insider information they're operating on.

My experience as a prosecutor has given me an understanding of how some criminals use the legal system for their own ends. Sometimes criminals will use a one-off arrest to get an attorney to file motions, so they can see who an informant is. I've seen other defense attorneys get pulled in unwittingly, thinking they're defending someone when they're really just part of a criminal's fact-finding mission. That's not some sweet lady's nephew: it's a setup. I don't want any part of that.

It's always best to avoid getting tangled up with the wrong people. Situations with angry exes, bad business deals, or criminal organizations are usually messy and can get out of control quickly.

Having a firm moral line in place will protect you in the long run.

EVALUATE YOURSELF, BECAUSE EVERYONE ELSE IS

Evaluation is fluid. It goes both ways. While you're trying to figure out if someone is bluffing or on track to win the hand, they're returning the favor.

Jury selection is a great illustration of this.

Jury trials are risky for both sides because you come to court with all your plans and witnesses, but there's a huge unknown variable that you can't control: the jury itself.

Depending on the nature of the case, there might be fifty or more random members from the community brought in for the prosecutor and defense to select a jury from.

The judge starts by asking each potential juror some questions. What's your name, are you married, do you have any kids, have you ever had any prior contact with law enforcement, do you know anything about the nature of the charges in this case that would make you unfit for this jury—basic things like that.

Any juror you can prove is biased, you can remove. You can also remove a set number of jurors for *any reason*. The people you're looking to remove are those who aren't a good fit for the case, or more accurately, not a good fit for *my* case.

Say I'm defending a gang member for a charge unrelated to gang activity. But I think his history with gangs will have a negative impact on the jury's evaluation of him, so I manage to keep the gang connection out of the case. The moment my client gets up on the stand and raises his arm, his gang tattoos are apparent. You know who would be really bad to have on the jury at that moment?

A retired law enforcement officer who worked in the gang unit. He knows what those tattoos are.

It's not always so obvious when it comes to choosing a juror, of course. Evaluating another person is never more of an art form than when it comes to choosing jurors. My goal is to figure out which people will be most responsive to the type of defense I'm using.

When I defended a young dad who had left his two kids in the car while he ran a quick errand, which turned into half an hour because of long lines, I wanted parents on the jury because they could relate to the situation I was going to present. They would know what it's like to be crazy busy and try to run errands with your children. People without kids wouldn't understand how you could possibly leave your kids in the car. On the other hand, I might get a parent who thought, "I would never leave my child in the car," and my juror choice could take a hard 180. I have to go with my gut instincts and try to figure out who is sympathetic.

> EVALUATING ANOTHER PERSON IS NEVER MORE OF AN ART FORM THAN WHEN IT COMES TO CHOOSING JURORS.

We're all being evaluated every day.

What you wear, your manner, how you handle yourself in a situation, the professional quality of your website and business card—everything is a cue someone else is picking up on and making a judgment about. They're using those cues to determine if you're credible, if you're legitimate, if you can be trusted.

You're doing this too.

You're looking at both obvious and subtle cues to try to get an understanding of a person or situation. Do I want to date this person? Do I want to get in on this business deal? Do I trust this person with a secret?

At first glance, the stabbing case at the cowboy bar seemed fairly simple. The woman's temper flared after seeing her ex, people got hurt, end of story.

But because I had put into place an evaluation process not only for what cases I would take, but how I would work them and decide on the best defense, the alleged victim's story was flipped on its head.

NOW THAT YOU'VE OPENED THE RIGHT DOOR . . .

Evaluation is just the start.

It helps you move from a no to a yes, but it doesn't completely direct you beyond that.

It's like going to a high-end foreign restaurant. You've evaluated the place by looking at online reviews. Friends have told you the food is to die for. It's in the nice part of town with a valet service and impeccable ambience. You decide to have a date night and go.

Evaluation got you in the door, but what happens when the server seats you and hands you a menu in a language you don't understand? You know you're going to order something, but will you accidentally order four appetizers and the wrong wine instead of the main course?

Evaluation helps you know whether to open the door, but knowing what to do once you get inside requires critical thinking skills. And that's where we're headed next.

CLOSING REMARKS

All action comes from evaluation.

Evaluating a situation is like preparing for a trip. What you pack and what maps you bring determine how the entire journey will go.

Always start your evaluation from a position of nonmovement and careful consideration before taking your first step. Sloppy or assumptive evaluation starts you down the wrong path from the beginning, and it's hard to get back on the right path after that.

Smart evaluation makes you ask yourself:

1. Does the action I'm about to take support my goals?
2. Can I evaluate the situation properly on my own?
3. Does the action have value?
4. What is the opportunity cost?
5. Does the action fit with my personal moral principles?

There should be no movement without careful evaluation first.

CHAPTER 3:
CRITICAL THINKING

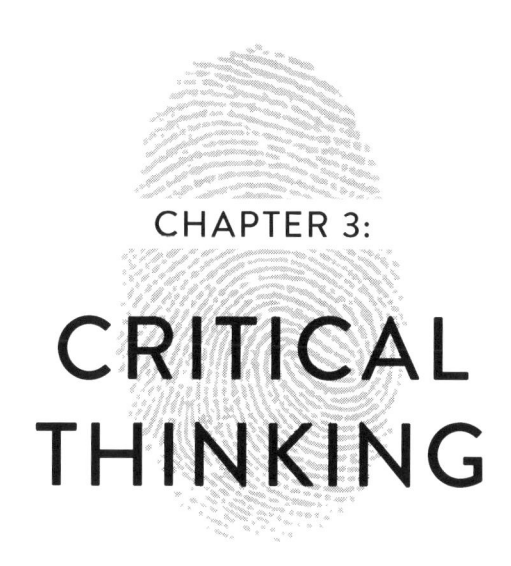

The guy could've used a shower. He smelled like a rough two days.

"Give me another," he slurred to the bartender.

The bartender shook his head, wiping down glasses behind the counter.

"I'm gonna have to cut you off, man," he said. "I think you've had enough."

The man was hunched over at the bar, shirt untucked with sweat stains growing under his arms. He'd been drowning himself in bottles for a few hours, staring at his smartphone. His eyes had that particular look of watery glass that comes with too much alcohol, mixed with a thousand-yard stare.

He pushed his nearly empty glass across the counter toward the bartender, hoping to change his mind. No luck. He stood up, catching his foot on the stool and headed for the door.

It was night, and the only light in the parking lot was a streetlamp at one end. Behind the bar was a junkyard with a high chain-link fence that ran along the edge of the entire property. On the other side of that fence were two pit bulls, dutifully guarding the metal scrap and discarded vehicle parts, barking every time someone exited the bar.

The man stood outside the bar for a few moments. Maybe he was trying to get his balance or figure out where he'd parked his car. It was a busy night, and each time people opened the door to the bar, loud music poured out into the parking lot, joined by the barking of the junkyard dogs.

It was amazing that, with all that racket going on, people heard the gunshots at all.

The story the man gave the police when they arrived on the scene was that he, still drunk, had fired his gun in self-defense.

"Those dogs," he'd said, waving vaguely toward the chain-link fence. "They got out and came at me. If I hadn't scared them off with my gun, I'd be dead right now."

Seeing that the dogs were still behind the fence, the police questioned the man on the details of the situation. "The dogs got through the fence somehow," he said, insisting they'd come across the parking lot toward him. "I fired my gun a couple of times, and they ran off."

When this case landed on my desk as a prosecutor, I knew it would be a challenge. It wasn't just because there weren't a lot of witnesses in the dark parking lot when the gunshots happened but because of who the man was.

He was an off-duty police officer.

The only other witness who saw anything outside the bar said that the man had been over by the fence where the dogs were. But it was dark and the witness had been on his way into the bar. He wasn't able to say anything with certainty. That wasn't much to go on.

The defense was going to run with the idea of self-defense and also play off the fact that he was a police officer to get some sympathy from the jury. Those could be solid approaches if done correctly, so I had to think critically about this case from both of those angles.

If I was going to show that self-defense was unlikely, the evidence presented would have to clearly show that to be the case. All reasonable doubt had to be removed, and the jury had to be sure that this man hadn't felt threatened.

Reasonable doubt can be created by an emotional response, and to combat that, I had to help the jury think critically instead of just emotionally when viewing the evidence presented. For this case, I created a timeline using witness statements and evidence.

After talking to the owner of the junkyard, I discovered that he chained his dogs up at 7 p.m., when he left for the night. He would unchain them when he came back to work the next morning. By reviewing witness statements made to the police, I determined the gunshots happened shortly before midnight. Witnesses in the bar, who called 911 to report the shots, said the defendant had left the bar around 11:45 p.m., and two surveillance cameras backed that up. That meant there was about a fifteen-minute gap between when he left and when the shots were fired. The exterior surveillance cameras didn't provide specific answers because the defendant couldn't be seen from their angle, though his car was visible. But even with the badly illuminated parking lot footage, you could see that no dogs were running around the parking lot. The only time the defendant showed up on the footage was when he appeared in frame walking to his car. He started to drive away right as the police cars pulled into the parking lot at about 12:05 a.m.

With this timeline, I could see that there was about fifteen minutes of unaccounted for time before the shooting and another five minutes of unaccounted for time after the shooting. What was he doing out in the parking lot for fifteen minutes before the shots were fired? Since he had a mobile phone, why didn't he ever call 911 about the pit bulls on the loose? Why wait another five minutes before driving away like nothing happened? With this timeline, the jury could see that several of the defendant's statements didn't align with his claim of self-defense.

> **VERIFIABLE FACTS CAN DISPEL CLAIMS OF SELF-DEFENSE, BUT THOSE SAME FACTS DON'T ALWAYS DISPEL EMOTION.**

I knew that if the defense was going to push the idea that this guy's job as a public servant was on the line, it would have serious emotional pull with the jury. Verifiable facts can dispel claims of self-defense, but those same facts don't always dispel emotion. Instead, I had to help the jury see through the emotional appeal.

Since the defense was going to focus on the fact that he was a police officer in an attempt for leniency, I decided I would also focus on the fact that he was a police officer but take a different angle. As a police officer, he was experienced with firearms. He knew safety procedures because he knew how dangerous firearms could be.

I'd take the defense's emotional appeal and redirect it. The jury could feel sorry for him that he was going to lose his job, or they could be upset with him for behaving in a way that he was trained to know was dangerous.

On the stand, I asked him questions about firearms and being under the influence.

"In order to become a police officer, were you required to complete a firearms safety course?"

"Yes," he said.

"And in that course, do they teach you how to safely handle a firearm?"

"Yes."

"Have other officers ever asked you to go shooting with them at the range?"

"Yes."

"Have you ever gone to the range with another officer who was visibly intoxicated?"

"No."

"Why not?"

"Because it's not safe for someone to go shooting while intoxicated."

"So does using a firearm while under the influence pose a risk to people?"

"Yes."

"Why?"

"Your reflexes and judgment are off . . ." he said, his voice trailing off.

I got him to admit it himself, that he should have known better. But we were just getting started. It was one thing to redirect the emotional appeal, but I had to prove beyond reasonable doubt that his self-defense claim was bogus.

I started by asking him questions that gave him a chance to reiterate his version of what had happened.

"I was outside the bar and suddenly I saw the pit bulls from the junkyard coming at me," he said. "So, I pulled my gun and fired it just to scare them off."

"How did the dogs get past the fence?" I asked.

"It was dark, so I couldn't really tell. I just saw them when they were coming across the parking lot and already through the fence."

"Would it surprise you to know that the junkyard owner chains up his dogs when he leaves at night, and that the next morning, his dogs were still on their chains?"

He paused. "I don't know. I just saw the dogs coming at me."

"The officers who responded the night of the shooting actually inspected that fence. And guess what? They didn't find any holes in the fence, no digging under the fence, and no unlocked gates. *So*, let me ask you again, how did the dogs get out?"

"I don't know."

"A witness saw you over by the fence. Were you ever at the fence?"

"Only for a little bit."

"What were you doing there?"

A few rounds of this kind of questioning, and the squirming defendant thoroughly destroyed the story of self-defense in the eyes of the jury. As it turns out, when you're drunk, teasing pit bulls from the safe side of a fence is a fun idea, and one way to get them really worked up is to fire your gun.

As an attorney, I want to help the jury strike the right balance between critical and emotional thinking. Yes, my goal is to persuade them to see my point of view and win—but the greater goal is a just verdict. (That's why, as a prosecutor, I never pushed a case to trial if I didn't believe I could prove the defendant was guilty beyond a reasonable doubt.) During a case, I want to present information in a way that encourages others to agree with what I believe the evidence shows. That buy-in comes through an emphasis on critical thinking with an appropriate level of emotional engagement. Critical thinking and emotional thinking are two sides of the same coin, and both have their place and purpose in proper evaluation. Too much of one or the other and your evaluation is likely to be off.

DEFYING PHYSICS AND LOGIC

It's not just at the trial level that critical thinking comes into play. From the very start of every case I prepare for, I have an entire process that I use. This is especially so when I get witness statements that seem impossibly colorful.

I had to prosecute an assault case that involved flying bricks at a construction site.

"She just started chucking bricks at me!" the victim said, the claims growing larger as the story went on. "It was like a hailstorm, there were so many bricks."

"But you weren't hit by any?"

"No, I managed to block them all."

"You blocked them all?"

"Well, I caught some of them," the victim said.

Bricks flying everywhere, not a single one landing a hit. Was this some kind of guerrilla baseball? Was this person like Neo from *The Matrix*, dodging bricks and popping back up for another round?

No one does that. No one morphs into a Hollywood action hero and blocks a barrage of bricks. You run, you duck, you hide, and you hope to God you don't get nailed in the head with a brick. The last thing you want is to end up like Marv in the 1992 film *Home Alone 2*.

The witness was emotionally convincing but factually lacking.

When a person starts telling these kinds of stories, whether it's egging on some pit bulls with a few gunshots or about their brick ninja skills, you have to home in on the language they're using to spot impossible or unlikely scenarios.

All. None. Always. Never. Everyone. No one.

These are words to watch out for because false stories often have no overlap. They're often composed of exclusionary extremes. False stories have perfect evil villains and perfect saintly victims. False stories sometimes feel more like a scene from a movie than real life. People describing heroic actions that defy the laws of physics or typical human responses should have their stories closely examined. Experience, mixed with critical thinking, helps you spot this kind of thing. An emotionally exciting story can fall apart under critical scrutiny.

A great example of this occurred in a city neighborhood during a summer heatwave.

The sun was mostly set, and streetlights were about all the light there was. Yelling and screaming trickled out from a small gray house on the corner of the street, and the neighbors standing outside chatting on the

FALSE STORIES HAVE PERFECT EVIL VILLAINS AND PERFECT SAINTLY VICTIMS.

sidewalk could hear a man and woman arguing. There was an awkwardness to the moment.

The door of the house flew open, and a man stormed outside. He quickly saw the group of people talking.

"What are you lookin' at?" he hollered, pausing for a moment before approaching the group with his hands waving.

From the corner of his eye, he later claimed, he could see something moving toward his head. He turned slightly, just enough to get a fist in his cheekbone, followed by a wad of spit.

He turned and pushed the man who had attacked him, and a fight started. There was more yelling and pushing, while the woman from inside the house screamed for everyone to stop. Eventually, the original punch-and-spit attacker returned with a baseball bat. He swung it around, slapping it against his hand, promising to use it.

The man rushed back to his house where the woman was still silhouetted against the door, the neighbors laughing and yelling insults at him as he retreated. He called 911, the police arrived to take his statement, and the man with the bat was eventually arrested and charged with assault and battery.

Seems cut-and-dried, right?

Except the story didn't ring true.

Further investigation and witness statements made the real story much clearer, starting with the physical stature of the victims. The man from the house, the alleged victim, was huge. We're talking extremely tall, solid, and several hundred pounds. The alleged attacker was a teenager who looked like a ninety-eight-pound weakling barely over five feet tall. It looked like a retelling of the story of David and Goliath, but there was nothing miraculous here.

Witnesses described a scary huge aggressor who had threatened them and put them in positions where they felt afraid for their safety. The screaming from inside the house had actually been part of a domestic assault, and the teenager, as it turned out, was a relative of the woman who had been the target of that assault. The alleged victim had gotten in a few punches of his own after the initial onslaught, and the scene was more like a Wild West brawl than one man getting beat up for no reason.

The alleged victim was more the perpetrator than anything.

Again, reviewing the evidence with a critical eye is what helps you get to the truth. Yet that's not the only application for critical thinking. It's more than evaluating evidence to determine what's plausible. It's also about how (or if) a case can be presented to a jury effectively.

Some cases are just difficult to deal with. You can critically think them to perfection, but it doesn't mean you want to try them. You have to decide if something is going to even make it to trial before worrying about how you'll try it.

For example, prostitution.

There are certain businesses that are known fronts for prostitution, and because cities don't like the seedy element they attract, law enforcement often targets them for stings. An officer would go in with a microphone in his shirt that provided a live feed and a recording, and the team would wait for him to say the code word that indicated something had happened that would be enough to arrest for prostitution.

It usually worked well, but there was a time or two when an officer would get so carried away that they didn't say the code word until it was all over.

Yeah.

This is not something that looks good in court when trying to prosecute these kinds of places for prostitution.

"Yes, members of the jury, your taxpayer dollars were used for this undercover operation that, uh, had an unplanned happy ending."

To make sting operation cases work, you have to be able to convince the jury of the need for undercover officers to help in the prosecution of some types of crimes. But with these kinds of failed scenarios, we usually had to find a way to resolve the case through a deal with the defendant because taking that recording and that oops-too-late ending to trial would not sit well with the jury.

Even if the undercover sting was perfect and the audio recording revealed prostitution was clearly on the menu, I had to be sure the jury I'd selected could handle what they were going to hear. As you can imagine, those recorded conversations got pretty colorful. Detailed. Descriptive. Graphic. Stuff that made you glad your mom wasn't in the room when the recording was played.

Some jury members wouldn't have a problem talking about the details of the case during deliberation, while others would rather crawl under a blanket than hear the recording, much less discuss it with eleven other strangers.

Whether it's guns going off in a bar or an undercover sting gone bad, critical thinking proves itself to be a journey and not a destination. Right from the beginning, there are many moving parts, much like a tumbler lock.

BREAKING OPEN THE LOCK

Sometimes you can walk right in the door and everything is there waiting for you. Lights are on, the furniture is in place, and dinner is on the table. That's the perfect case where you can take the jury right to the conclusion.

Sometimes the door is locked. Short of brutally kicking the door down and making an embarrassing scene, you have to find a different way to get in. You need a key.

This is where the tumbler lock comes into play. A pin-and-tumbler lock has pins at various lengths and will only release when these pins are pushed to the correct position. A key works because it gets the tumblers in a lock to line up correctly. They don't have to line up in a perfectly straight line; they just have to be arranged in the pattern that is set to release the lock.

If you have the right key, what was locked can be unlocked.

The right key might be a specific key for the lock, or it could be a master key that unlocks everything in the building. For some cases, I might not have the specific key to unlock the win (that perfect piece of evidence) but instead, I can use the master key approach of helping the jury think the way I want them to.

Remember, I'm dealing with emotions and a conflicting presentation of facts from the other side. I need to make sure what I do lines everything up to unlock the right conclusion. I line up the evidence and facts so that the jury is pointed to only one reasonable conclusion—the one supported by the facts, and coincidentally, the one I want them to make.

There are times when the pins don't all line up, though, and the door stays locked. The one sure obstacle to critical thinking, whether it's my own efforts during preparation or what I'm trying to help a jury see, is confirmation bias.

CONFIRMATION BIAS IS THE TRAP

We all face hundreds of decisions every day.

When decision fatigue sets in, we go for the cheapest, easiest solution. It's how others can take advantage of us, yet it tends to be our fallback approach because making logical decisions and conclusions takes a lot of energy. It's easier to revert to something we already know.

It's no different with a jury.

There's a difference between leading the jury to a logical conclusion and reinforcing confirmation bias. Confirmation bias is when we perceive and understand information based on what we already know and believe. We see what we expect to see. We rely only on emotional thinking instead of using critical thinking. The same facts can paint two very different pictures depending on whether you use the brush of emotional thinking or critical thinking.

An emotional response can be a good thing if it sells the jury on the story I'm telling. A cold-blooded murderer could also be a father protecting his family. A greedy thief could be a mother trying to feed her family. The cases I deal with are emotionally charged. There are fights, sexual assault, marriage issues, murder—being objective and logical isn't easy.

When I build a case, I can't put my emotions into it, because not only would that be exhausting, it would also blind me. I can easily get so emotionally invested in a case that I stop thinking critically. I stop asking the tough questions I need to be asking. Does this make sense? Did this really happen? Am I assuming something about my client? Emotion helps create confirmation bias.

Don't get me wrong—emotional thinking has its place, just like logical thinking. All Spock and no Kirk won't get you anywhere with people, because, as I pointed out, most people are making decisions based on their emotions. You can't avoid the reality that people are probably 80 percent emotional and 20 percent logical when it comes to the conclusions they're making. If you fail to engage their emotions, you fail to persuade. I want my jury to buy-in to the emotions I'm directing them to, and then I want to provide them a logical and safe way to get past any roadblocks and to the emotional destination they now want.

The key point is that when I prepare a case, I have to make my own conclusions about what's happening using critical thinking, free from emotion. The argument I build should be logical. I have to look at the facts and evidence on their own basis without my emotions coloring my understanding. I have to make sure the evidence supports the story I've been told. A fake story, no matter how emotionally powerful, is indefensible.

If I go in with preconceived notions, I only head in one direction from the start. All my great work is still wrong because I've been off course the whole time. It's like when you're out for a drive. If you start looking off to the side, you start drifting out of your lane.

Most of us naturally have biases we revert to in life out of habit or as a defense mechanism, but as a trial lawyer, I don't have the luxury of confirmation bias, because it leads to tunnel vision. You see what you want to see. You only find what you're looking for. The only facts you recognize are those in the tunnel you're trapped in. As a trial lawyer, if I develop tunnel vision early on in the case, I'm going to be unprepared for surprises that pop up during the trial.

> IF I GO IN WITH PRECONCEIVED NOTIONS, I ONLY HEAD IN ONE DIRECTION FROM THE START.

I know that some cases arrive on my desk with tunnel vision built in. Prosecutors and police officers have a tendency for tunnel vision because confirmation bias sets them on that narrow path. For example, they often assume that the first person to call the police, or claim they have been assaulted, is the victim. That's confirmation bias. Their whole case is based on that first assumption.

Consider a hypothetical domestic assault case. The 911 call seems pretty clear to anyone who hears it. A woman describes a fight she's had with her husband that left her with some kind of injury. She says that he started the fight, then drove off in his truck and now she's home alone. According to her, the fight started in the house and moved outside to the front porch.

When the police arrive, they take the woman's statement. She has a scratch on her neck. The husband isn't there. Her story seems to line up, and everything seems legit. Then the husband pulls up in his truck, arriving back on the scene.

"Your wife says you hit her," the police tell him.

"She's full of shit," he says. "I'm not saying anything."

Of course he would say she was lying, but is there truth to the little that he said? Was he even there to have the fight? Did he start the fight? Did everything happen as the wife described? Was she the victim? As a lawyer, I can't assume he's lying just because his wife made the call and it looks like her story fits.

I've seen it many times as a prosecutor. Maybe they have a custody case and they want to hurt the ex. Maybe emotions ran high during an argument and they want some payback. Whatever the reason, some people know how to use the system, and because I know this is true, I have to aggressively refuse to develop confirmation bias right at the start of a case. I can't assume the one who called the police is the victim.

I can look at the criminal history of the people involved. I can talk to them and ask questions that get beneath the surface. I can review the evidence to see if things add up. Maybe, for example, that fighting couple have a Ring camera installed by their door, and I can end the debate easily.

For me, developing a framework of skepticism is crucial. I have to always ask myself if things are what they seem. You don't have to be pessimistic about everything, but you do have to develop an inward habit of challenging what you're seeing and hearing, and asking basic questions that require the claims to prove themselves to you.

Using this approach with the hypothetical domestic assault case means that maybe the husband didn't start the fight. The Ring camera showed there was no fight in the front yard, and the scratch isn't visible on the wife's neck as she's screaming obscenities at the truck disappearing down the street. The husband was right, but he didn't want to say anything to get his wife in trouble. Obvious domestic assault turns into something else entirely by rejecting confirmation bias early on.

Of course, doing that for my own case preparation is one thing. Preparing a case in a way that helps the jury avoid confirmation bias is another thing entirely.

For starters, I try to disprove my own conclusion. I know how I plan on proving it, but how could I disprove it?

Understanding the players and the roles helps. Seasoned prosecutors learn to attack their own case from many angles because they have to fortify it against every attack. The defense doesn't need to do that. They simply need to get one foot in the door and it's enough for that reasonable doubt. One bonus from coming at your own case from several angles is that you'll probably find more than one way to get to your objective. That means a much stronger case.

The next thing to do is to examine all the different ways we might fail.

Startups in Silicon Valley use the premortem approach before launching a new product. Everyone assumes they've built the best possible product, and they assume it'll be wildly successful and everyone will love it as much as they do.

But those assumptions are the weak spot. Those assumptions are used to make decisions that lead to conclusions, and they are pure confirmation bias. A premortem asks why something failed, even though it hasn't yet. It's a way to find all the holes and gaps.

It's different from disproving conclusions because it puts to death the assumptions that helped you arrive at those conclusions. Attacking your case from all angles helps you defend what you have, but a premortem helps you delve into the *validity* of what you have. It assumes what you have is on the road to being dead on arrival. It asks "why did this fail?" instead of "how might my right idea be attacked?"

There's a process of elimination at work in both of these steps, and it's a process that requires incredibly (and often painfully) honest answers and serious critical thinking. Only after you've torn down your argument and made sure it's rebuilt to be better are you ready to travel on.

GET OFF THE PAVED PATH

Imagine an Ivy League college, brick buildings surrounded by trees, with manicured lawns and tidy sidewalks connecting the buildings together. Some sidewalks angle across the quad, perhaps, but there is an orderliness to everything. From a bird's eye view, the sidewalks make sense and are logically placed, connecting point A to point B.

But once you get on the ground, you notice something else at work.

Cutting across the nice lawns and through the bushes and trees are crude, well-worn dirt paths. Is this an assault against the logic of the sidewalks? Do the students have no respect for the landscaping? Or is it evidence that the obvious path isn't always the best path?

When you come to a dirt path on campus, take it.

The dirt paths in college are the paths people are actually using. They're the fastest route, and they get you where you need to go. The sidewalks won't always get you to your destination as quickly, and sometimes, speed matters. When it comes to trying a case, taking the longer route or lingering too long is a good way to lose.

You can win a war of attrition, but why would you want to?

Bit by bit, over great lengths of time, you can wear an enemy down until they finally collapse simply from exhaustion. As a defense attorney, I can topple the tower the prosecution built, one paper cut at a time, but that has to be a last resort. I would rather have one solid defense, one missile, to bring that tower down than chip away at the base of it over and over. A solid defense is the shortest and fastest route to victory.

A war of attrition has great cost for the victor.

If I take that approach, I run the risk of losing the case, losing the jury, and losing my focus. The longer a case drags out, the more time, money, and personal energy I'm wasting. The longer you linger in one place, the more you sink and get bogged down.

Speed is crucial in a battle.

At the start of the American Civil War, it was clear people thought it would be over quickly. They showed up at the First Battle of Bull Run with blankets and picnic baskets, thinking they were going to watch an afternoon of shooting. But two years into the war, people's ideas had changed. The war was a slog, dragging out and draining the nation. The people's enthusiasm was drained to almost nothing.

Now you have the problem of how to re-engage. When something has been drawn out, how do you get people back to being interested, to caring?

Timing is part of critical thinking.

You might know you have to make a big statement or bold move, but your timing has to be perfect. Otherwise, you'll get far less bang for your buck.

A SOLID DEFENSE IS THE SHORTEST AND FASTEST ROUTE TO VICTORY.

President Lincoln understood this. He knew that the Emancipation Proclamation would reinvigorate people, and he had it ready to go, but he also knew he had to get the timing right. Signing it after a series of heavy losses would overwhelm an already exhausted people who were growing tired of the war. They were losing loved ones in the fighting, there was fear and financial struggles, and now they were supposed to take on another cause?

But then the North won a much needed victory at Antietam in September of 1862. The Southern Army had been winning battles and invading the North, but the victory at Antietam forced the invading Southern Army to retreat from Northern territory.

Lincoln knew this was the perfect time.

He signed the Emancipation Proclamation just five days after the North's victory at Antietam and, in that moment, gave the people of the North purpose again.

In November of 1863, Lincoln again capitalized on the perfect time to deliver an inspiring message for the people of the North. Four months prior, on the July 4th weekend, the North took the southern city of Vicksburg, knocking three southern states out of the war and giving the North control over the entire Mississippi River. That same weekend, the North defeated the Southern Army at Gettysburg, forcing them to retreat from the North for good.

Months after those battles, President Lincoln was asked to speak at the dedication of the new cemetery in Gettysburg, which served as the final resting place for so many fallen soldiers. At that dedication, Lincoln gave a two-minute, awe-inspiring speech that still impacts us today, over 150 years later. The crowd pressed in on all sides, listening to Lincoln memorialize a key moment in our nation's history:

> *It is for us the living, rather, to be dedicated here to the unfinished work which they who fought here have . . . so nobly advanced. . . . [We] here highly resolve that these dead shall not have died in vain—that this nation, under God, shall have a new birth of freedom—and that government of the people, by the people, for the people, shall not perish from the earth.*

Lincoln had perfect timing down. He knew exactly when these powerful messages would mean the most, even if he didn't fully understand at the time just how perfect his timing was or what the impact of his speech would be.

He wasn't the only American president to understand the importance of perfect timing. On June 12, 1987, President Reagan stood at a podium in front of the Brandenburg Gate in West Berlin, about to deliver a now-famous speech. A crowd waving American and German flags cheered in front of him, while West Germany's Chancellor Helmut Kohl, who would later help reunite Germany, was seated to the left.

Framing the Berlin Wall as an emblem of division preventing human liberty across not only Europe but across the world, Reagan specifically addressed General Secretary Mikhail Gorbachev.

"Mr. Gorbachev, tear down this wall!"

It was a huge risk to make that demand, but Reagan was capitalizing on a wave of sentiment that would eventually free up Eastern Europe from Soviet influence and unify Germany. Like Lincoln, he was already prepared to make the statement. He knew it had to be said. He was simply waiting for the right time and the right place to say it.

Reagan could have said the same thing at a press conference at the White House, and Lincoln could have signed the Emancipation Proclamation earlier. Both presidents were prepared and able to do so. But getting the timing right is a significant part of critical thinking, and they knew it.

You don't have to be a president to put this to work for you. I had to prosecute a case involving prostitution where we had the audio recordings from a sting operation. While the defendant insisted she had only agreed to give a massage, I had the recordings and transcripts from the phone call she had with our undercover officer.

It had not been a conversation about a massage. The recordings were so detailed and raunchy that the first time they were played for me before the trial, the officer had to take his phone off speaker because the others in the room were struggling to control their reactions to what was being said.

On the stand during the trial, the defendant continued to swear it was only a massage, and she was very convincing. But I had those recordings ready to go. I continued to question her and let her lead the jury through her story. Then at the right moment, when it seemed as if she'd convinced people of her innocence, I played the recordings for the jury. They were devastating to her claims. Playing the recordings after her testimony was more powerful than playing them at the beginning. It allowed her to firmly and emphatically establish a story that was proven entirely false in just a few minutes.

Timing is knowing when to turn the key that unlocks the door.

TAKE THE ROAD LESS TRAVELED

Back in the 1990s, when email was just starting to become popular, Hotmail was struggling to get new users to adopt their platform. In six months, they'd managed to get a million users, but things had plateaued. They needed exponential growth to survive.

They used all the recommended methods for growing a business. They put up billboards. They took out ads.

Nothing was working.

At their wit's end, with the death bell about to toll, creative thinkers at Hotmail decided to try something unusual.

"What if we made our users ambassadors?" they asked. "What if our product itself became the vehicle to get others to sign up to use it?"

They decided to tuck "PS: I love you. Get your free email at Hotmail" at the end of every email, linking back to the sign-up page for Hotmail. Free email accounts weren't standard at the time, so arriving on a registration page with the ability to have a new, non-ISP email account in just a few minutes was unique.

With this new approach, their user base doubled in five weeks. A year later, when Microsoft bought the company, Hotmail had over 400 million users. It seemed as if everyone had a Hotmail account.

Creative thinking saved the company and blazed a trail for future startups. That approach has been used for more than growing companies, though. It has also helped win wars.

During World War II, the Allies came to know Europe as Fortress Europe. The Nazis had such control that it seemed certain no one could penetrate their defenses.

CRITICAL THINKING REQUIRES CREATIVE THINKING IF YOU WANT IT TO GO ANYWHERE.

But the Allies also knew that Hitler was terrified of General George S. Patton, who he thought was one of the best generals around. So, they brought Patton to Britain, setting him up with fake tanks and decoys of every sort, so it would seem as if the invasion force was coming from his location. Yet the real invasion was planned for another location. When the Allies landed at Normandy, the Germans were caught off guard. Once on the European continent, the Allies used a similar approach through what was known as the Ghost Army, employing blow-up tanks and guns, fake radio transmissions, and audio recordings simulating massive deployments to distract from reality.

Critical thinking allowed the Allies to come up with a solution to the problem they were facing on how to successfully invade Fortress Europe. They knew they should capitalize on Hitler's fear of Patton, and on the German Army's expectation of the Allied troop movement. But it was creative thinking that provided the solution.

And that's the key: critical thinking requires creative thinking if you want it to go anywhere. How do I package up the evidence I have and make it all work? How do I use this information to my advantage?

Critical thinking and creative thinking go hand in hand because critical thinking is the gateway to innovation. When a new precedent is set, it means it was something that hadn't been done before. Someone has thought outside the box, trying to solve a problem in their case. All of a sudden, there is a new precedent that others can use to build their cases. Without this process, the law would stay stagnant.

Critical thinking is the art of plotting a course to take people on a journey so everyone arrives at the same destination. Creative thinking is knowing which vehicle to use on that journey. That's why creative thinking must be part of critical thinking.

As the saying goes, good ideas are always crazy until they're not.

PROCESS LEADS TO DESTINATIONS

Critical thinking, in the art of negotiation and winning cases, isn't a stand-alone action. It's a process.

Consider the jury. With a jury, you have people from all demographics and walks of life. They aren't all going to immediately jump on board with my theory of the case. I can't walk in on jury selection day and start making my argument. I have to follow the process. I have to build my credibility in front of them with how I've evaluated and prepared the case. I have to help them think critically in how I argue it.

When you're negotiating with someone, and you've done all this foundational work and led them down a path of critical thinking to the conclusion you want, you're at the moment of buy-in.

You tell Gorbachev to tear down the wall. You release the Emancipation Proclamation. You state your closing argument.

Don't let this guilty man go free.

Don't convict an innocent woman.

I've learned that when I get this process right, the jury can reach the right conclusion on their own. There's nothing more powerful than when they arrive at that conclusion themselves without explanation. In that moment, persuasion is easy.

> WHEN YOU ONLY LOOK AT THINGS TO PROVE YOUR POINT, YOU LOSE.

When you only look at things to prove your point, you lose. You're open to attack, and you never take people on the journey to reach the same conclusion on their own.

Build your case on critical thinking. Establish credibility through solid evaluation. Come up with a creative solution to get people on the right path.

Without this approach, all your future preparation will eventually fail.

CLOSING REMARKS

Critical thinking is the art of devising a way for people to follow you on a journey so that everyone arrives at the same destination: the destination you are hoping for. But you have to do your own critical thinking before you can help others down the same path.

Ask yourself questions like:

1. Am I operating with confirmation bias or under assumptions?
2. Do my theories have holes?

3. Do I have logical and sound answers for those who question my conclusions?
4. Do I know how emotions might be affecting the outcome, and how (or if) I should harness them?

Once you're in a solid position, you can then use critical thinking to get those you're trying to persuade to ask the right questions. You can use critical thinking to uncover the problems that need to be solved *creatively*.

Critical thinking cuts through the distracting clutter and gets everyone to the desired destination together.

CHAPTER 4:

PREPARING

The sun was dropping fast when the police arrived on the scene. On the edge of a parking lot, alongside swing sets, walking paths, and a basketball court, was a woman lying across the ground. She looked like a broken doll, cuts and bloody bruises visible. She wasn't dead yet, but she was on her way if medical help didn't act quickly.

As the ambulance loaded up the victim, the police began piecing together the story from those at the scene, all of whom were distraught or angry, and some of whom had minor injuries of their own. All that was clear was that a woman had been run over by a car. What was unclear was the *why* and the *who*.

Although grainy, a gas station surveillance camera across the street caught the entire event on video. The footage showed a car with two people inside driving toward a handful of people in the parking lot. Neither the driver nor the passenger could be identified except for a large tattoo on the passenger's arm, draped outside the car's open window. It was obviously a man's arm, but the tattoo itself wasn't clear.

The car cruised to a stop in front of the group of people, and a shouting match ensued. Suddenly, the car lurched forward toward the group of people. Everyone scattered except the girl. The car plowed into her, launching her onto the hood of the car. The car jerked, she rolled off onto the ground, and the mystery driver and passenger sped away.

The prosecutor tried to work backward from what was known, using some assumptions. Who was friends with whom at the scene? Who had any motive to commit this crime? Who did the car belong to? It was the kind of speculation that might give you some persons of interest but no real evidence you can build a case on.

The police had almost no leads until they tracked down the registered owner of the car used for the assault. As it turned out, the registered owner had a lengthy criminal record with several open felony drug sales cases of his own. He also had some information he was happy to share with the police.

"I didn't run that lady over at the park. I was in Vegas when that happened. But I know who did it," he told them.

Apparently, this witness had sold his car to my client, the defendant, who he alleged was the driver of the car when it plowed into the group of people at the park. According to the witness, my client and a friend showed up earlier that day, bought the car, and then the witness overheard my client talking on the phone before he left.

"I just bought a dope new car. She's gonna be so surprised when I meet her at the park in a few hours. I'm going to flatten her." As it happens, my client was an ex-boyfriend of the victim that was run over.

Within a few minutes, the police had the name of my client, a motive, and a statement that didn't do my client any favors. It was enough to get a search warrant and put my client in serious hot water.

But there were problems with the case against my client.

For starters, witnesses who have their own criminal cases pending aren't always reliable. Every once in a while, they're looking to make a deal and will tell law enforcement what they think they want to hear in the hopes that it might benefit their own pending cases. So, how credible was this witness that allegedly sold the car to my client? The supposed phone call couldn't be verified. And who discusses their plans for committing a serious crime in front of someone they barely know? Why would anyone spend money to buy a new car they plan on damaging a few hours later?

People don't intentionally wreck what they just bought—especially when they're proud of the purchase.

Another issue was that my client obviously knew the woman that was hit with the car, so he should have been easy for her to recognize. Yet the woman and the other witnesses at the scene, who were friends of the woman and would have seen her with her ex-boyfriend in the past, had specifically said they did not recognize the driver and that they could not see the passenger. So, the only identification was my client allegedly talking about his plan to commit the crime earlier in the day in front of a person he barely knew. Still another inconsistency was that my client had an elbow tattoo that resembled the one visible in the surveillance video—which would potentially have made him the passenger. Given these meager facts, I immediately realized the prosecutor had a paper-thin case, even though it looked good on the surface.

My client had a temper and some past convictions for violent crimes. He also had threatened his ex-girlfriend when they broke up a few weeks prior to the incident, saying that if he couldn't have her, no one could. These were problematic things to be sure, but not enough, in my opinion, to be prosecuting someone for attempted murder.

The prosecutor had two glaring problems. The first was that the proof tying my client to the incident was weak. The second was that even if the prosecutor could convince a jury that my client was the driver of the car, the prosecutor still had to prove that my client intended to kill the victim. My client was being charged with attempted murder, which means the prosecutor had to prove my client *intended* to murder the victim. It was a question of intent.

You know what's easier to prove than attempted murder? Actual murder. Intent to kill is a lot easier to prove when someone actually dies. When no one dies, trying to prove intent to kill requires a lot more work, and that proof was pretty much absent in the case against my client. Even if you believed he was driving the car, you still had to prove intent to kill.

The surveillance footage from the gas station didn't show the complete incident. You could see the car heading toward the group of people standing at the edge of the parking lot near the road. Then it slowed down in front of the people in the parking lot, and there was a brief verbal exchange between the bystanders and either the driver or the passenger, or both. Then the driver accelerated out of the parking lot, hitting the female bystander on his way out. It was obvious that the car swerved in her direction before hitting her. The car never stopped or slowed after hitting her; it just quickly drove away out of the parking lot. This obviously raised a lot of questions about intent.

If he was the driver and intended to kill his ex-girlfriend, why did he stop in the parking lot at all? Did he only intend to scare her? Did he merely intend to hit her with the car but not kill her? Did she say or do something that caused him to think he had to hit her for his own safety?

Yes, the prosecutor was going to have a hell of a time proving this case. It felt like a case of convenience without much substance. My client made a convenient defendant, but the evidence was based on a lot of assumptions rather than hard evidence.

There was so much involved in the case, from surveillance video and witness statements to digging into the elements of the law involving murder and attempted murder cases.

Preparation was the key.

THE TRUTH, FROM TWELVE DIFFERENT ANGLES

Before I left the DA's office, I had to prepare a murder case where the whole thing was caught on video. That seemed like a no-brainer. Play the video and hear the jury sing guilty.

But the defense was still going to make arguments, proposing and questioning everything from self-defense to intent. As a prosecutor, I had to dissect the video to prepare for every argument that could be made.

I decided to have a technician at the DA's office make a more watchable movie of the footage because there were twelve different camera angles, which could make it difficult for the jury to follow the action. Creating that video was incredibly labor-intensive, but it was useful to keep witnesses from going sideways on the stand. They weren't going to change their story when the video would show they were lying. Even more importantly, it helped to answer questions that might pop up in the jurors' minds since it played out like a movie.

No matter how obvious the outcome seemed, even with everything caught on video, I had to be prepared to provide evidence supporting my case and to deflect whatever the defense might try to use to poke holes in my case.

Another case I prosecuted involved a parking violation. It wasn't murder, but I still needed to be well-prepared.

"Would you be interested in giving my client a deal?" the defense attorney asked me.

"No deal. I've got this. I'm good to go."

And I was.

A man worked part-time as a mechanic across town in an area where parking was all but impossible. The few parking spots that were available were metered. The only exception was for handicapped parking areas, which prompted this fellow to use his wife's handicapped placard when he went to work.

Prime parking. No cost. Low fuss. Completely illegal.

If he was driving his wife around, that would be fine. As long as the person to whom the placard is issued is in the vehicle, it's not a problem. So as I prepared to prosecute this case, I knew the defense would try to say that the wife was with him or that he would be picking her up.

Getting the work schedule from his employer would be the proof I needed. I'd subpoena his employer, get the work schedule, and get someone from his job to come in and testify about that schedule. I even got a map of the area to show the likelihood of that parking spot being anything but a quick place to get to work. The goal was to show that he was parking there a few minutes before he was due to clock in and not there to meet his wife.

I knew the defense would bring in the defendant's wife. He did. It was hard to watch. She was obviously trying to cover for her husband but having a hard time explaining why she'd be going to work with him. The guy was a mechanic. There was no reason a woman in a wheelchair would be spending half a day parked in front of a strip mall near an auto repair shop when she lived and worked across town.

By being prepared with the map and the work schedule, I boxed him in. I won that case.

The showdown between a prosecutor and a defense attorney is one completely based on preparation. Each shot is fired until there's none that can be returned. You lose if you're not prepared.

Here's the tricky bit, though. When you go into the case knowing there are some things you're not specifically prepared for, you're in better shape than if you go in foolishly thinking you've covered all the bases.

> YOU LOSE IF YOU'RE NOT PREPARED.

As a defense attorney, I don't always know what evidence the prosecution will put forward and how they'll present it. My preparation beforehand includes being ready to adapt to whatever pops up during the trial.

But if you go into a situation thinking you're completely prepared and are suddenly forced to realize you're not, it's hard to get your heart beating again.

I know from experience. Take this next case I prosecuted, for instance.

DRUNKEN CARS DON'T DRIVE THEMSELVES

The guy had a habit of driving drunk, and someone finally called it in one evening. That someone was an employee of the drunk driver. The employee called 911, saying he had recognized his boss's car pull out of the neighborhood sports bar and drive a mile before pulling into his driveway and parking his car partially on the lawn. Not long after, police found the guy reeking of alcohol, sitting in his haphazardly parked car with two wheels digging into his lawn. The case seemed like an easy win.

But I wanted to be prepared. So I contacted the witness.

"You saw the guy?" I asked.

"Yep."

"You know it was him?"

"Yep. He's my boss, and I saw him park his car in front of his house. I know it was his house because I live just a few streets down and I've been to his place several times before."

"You recognized his vehicle?"

"Yep. If his car isn't in the parking lot at work, it's either at that sports bar or parked in front of his house. He's always driving drunk."

It seems obvious, but to prove someone was driving under the influence of alcohol, you have to prove they were driving; and while they were driving, they were under the influence. I had the witness who said he saw the guy, and I had the blood alcohol tests that said he was definitely under the influence.

After speaking with the witness, I felt like I was good to go. I tried to resolve the case through a plea deal, but the defendant was not willing to plead guilty. So, the case progressed all the way to trial. During the trial, I called the witness to the stand.

"What were you doing that day?" I asked.

"I was out running errands," the witness answered.

"Are you familiar with the defendant?"

"Yep. He's my boss."

"Is he in court?"

"Yep, right there," the witness said, pointing to the defendant.

"Did you see him driving that day?"

"No, I saw his car parked halfway into his lawn when I drove by his house."

Now this was something I hadn't prepared for.

"But did you see him driving home from the sports bar before you saw his car parked in his driveway?"

"No, I saw him in the front yard of his house."

"When you called 911, you said you saw him driving his vehicle while leaving the sports bar, and you said you thought he was driving drunk because he was swerving a lot. Is that what you saw?"

"No."

The witness looked down. My heart sank.

All of this while on the stand, in front of the jury.

Crap.

Maybe he saw him driving, maybe he didn't; but he basically injected too much reasonable doubt into the case. There was almost no chance the jury was going to convict. The witness had either just committed perjury by lying under oath, or he just admitted to falsely filing a police report while under oath on the stand. Either way, his credibility was shot, and so was my case.

One minute earlier I was totally prepared. And prepared to win. But that was gone. I was going to lose. It was barely ten minutes into the trial and I had to ask the judge for a recess. I knew the case wasn't winnable anymore, and even if I could present a reason for why the witness was lying, the case was over.

I thought I was prepared, so I hadn't gathered any other corroborating evidence to show the defendant was driving. I hadn't gotten any surveillance footage. I didn't have other witnesses lined up. The arresting officer hadn't done any investigation, like checking the hood of the car to see if it was hot, because he had a witness statement.

As it turns out, I wasn't prepared at all. The moment the witness went sideways, I realized I had nothing ready to counter it. I should have been more prepared. I should have realized that my star witness might have a motive to either lie or change his original story. The defendant was his boss, after all. Talk about an awkward situation. Yet I completely overlooked that fact when I was preparing the case, and it cost me. The witness probably did see his boss driving, but then changed his story when he realized that he wasn't going to remain anonymous and would actually have to testify against his boss in open court.

INSTANT LUCK IS USUALLY YEARS IN THE MAKING

If you're not prepared, you lose.

You might get the best of a situation and come out on top, but you didn't emerge without damage. It's a winning loss. I know what it's like to win a case, like this next one, but lose in other important ways.

It seemed like a standard burglary case at a pawn shop. This shop happened to handle coins and precious metals, which explained the heavily barred windows and attempts at security. There was lots of evidence, some witnesses, and a likely conviction. But as I interviewed the police officer on the stand, I decided on a whim to take a route of questioning that would help the jury understand the magnitude of the theft. I wanted to show that this wasn't just a few odds and ends that walked out the door, but something with real payout for the defendant.

"How much gold was stolen from the shop?" I asked.

The officer told me.

"How much does an ounce of gold go for?"

The officer told me.

"So how much would the entire amount be worth?"

The officer did not tell me because he didn't know off the top of the head.

I had put a question out that really didn't need to be answered, but now it was hanging in the air for the jury to see, no answer in sight. This was bad.

I quickly scrounged around for a calculator to do the math right there in front of the jury, feeling ridiculous as I struggled to convert pounds to ounces and then do multiplication with every eye on me. I had never heard a courtroom clock tick so loudly.

Yes, I won the case. But the embarrassment stuck with me. You want to be in control at all times, and I wasn't in control at that moment. Looking incompetent really isn't a win. Losing face can be as bad as losing a case.

What I learned that day was that you don't ask a question you're not prepared to answer. Don't make a decision you're not prepared for. And don't trust luck to fill in the gaps if you go ahead and do both of those things anyway.

People like to talk about how a lucky break is what it takes to succeed, but the reality is that success has nothing to do with luck. It's not up to chance. As Louis Pasteur once said, "Chance favors the prepared mind."

Lucky breaks tend to happen after years of hard work. When your big moment drops in your lap, you'd better be prepared, or it won't be your big moment of success. It will be a big moment of failure or a missed opportunity. Any time I find a piece of evidence that blows open a case, I didn't get lucky. I put in the work. And when I ask a question I wasn't prepared for, I'm trusting luck to come through, knowing that luck actually has a terrible track record.

The more prepared person is always going to take control of a situation. They can outperform the person who's smarter or more naturally gifted. When I know what will be argued, I have my response prepared. I'm ready to play a game my opponent might not even know is about to start.

IF SOMEONE ASKS YOU TO PLAY A GAME OF CHECKERS, ALSO BE READY TO PLAY CHESS.

If someone asks you to play a game of checkers, also be ready to play chess. Prepare beyond what you think you'll have to play.

PREPARATION DEPENDS ON YOUR ROLE

You can approach preparation using a system, as long as you know your role in that moment. Different roles mean different goals.

PREP AS A PROSECUTOR

As a prosecutor, I prepared for each case the same way.

I start with evaluation. You've probably heard of SWOT, which stands for strengths, weaknesses, opportunities, and threats. A SWOT analysis is simply assessing those four aspects, and that's basically what I'd do.

As soon as I'd get a case, I'd read the police reports, and then look at the accused's criminal history for possible exposure to attack. I'd look at what charges were made and try to get a general feel for the case. At that point, I'd determine what the case is worth. That means I'd decide what kind of offers I'd be willing to make and what deals I'd be willing to accept. What offers I'd make compared to what deals I'd accept aren't always the same; there's a gap there to leave room for negotiations. Then I'd look for problems in the case and figure out how to fix them.

It's here that I'd get to my first fork in the road: is this case going to resolve? If the answer is no, I have to prepare for trial.

Trial preparation for prosecution starts with lining up my witnesses. Without witnesses, there's no trial. I have to look for any problems with my witnesses that might come up at trial and make sure my subpoenas were sent out and acknowledged. Then I make sure I have my evidence or other exhibits, like photos, ready to go for use in court. If there are audio recordings, I want to be sure they're transcribed. Some of these things, such as the list of witnesses and exhibits, have to be given to the defense attorney.

From there, I'm going to prepare my trial brief, which is my summary of the case that the judge will read, as well as drafting the motions I want. Before the trial starts, I want to be clear on things like who's qualified as an expert and what statements will be coming in.

As a prosecutor, you're required to disclose all exculpatory evidence, which is any evidence that could show the defendant might not be guilty.

That evidence needs to be turned over to the defense. When prosecuting a case, I was careful to never withhold anything from the defense, not even if a witness had something problematic in their past. Prior to the trial, I knew I could always argue whether that evidence was relevant and admissible.

From the case preparation, I move on to issues involving the jury who will be deciding the case.

I decide what jury instructions I want the judge to read. I determine what kind of jurors would be good for this case, and come up with questions that hit on the topics and themes that will help me choose jurors who will be receptive to the case I'm making.

For example, if criminal threats are part of the case, I might ask a potential juror to tell me how a person could be harmed. I want to see if they agree that it can be physical, emotional, or financial. I want to see if they're on board with the idea that not all harm is the same, that you don't have to be bleeding to be considered harmed.

Depending on the case, I need to find out if they're going to be OK with the types of evidence that might be presented, whether it's photos of a murder crime scene or hearing the audio of someone soliciting sex. I want to get this all done up front because I don't want a juror caught off guard during the trial, distracted by the evidence and functioning in a state of emotion that keeps them from hearing the facts of the case.

I also want to watch out for jurors that might not get along because, as a prosecutor, I want twelve people who will be decisive, not divisive. I remember one situation where, during the jury selection process, a woman from Eastern Europe spoke strongly in support of legalizing the crime we'd be prosecuting.

"That way, you can tax it and people can make money and everybody wins," she said with zero shame.

The potential jurors around her looked at her as if she'd sprouted horns, so I knew I didn't want her on the jury. She'd only create conflict and keep the group from coming to a decision together. Anyone who has a divisive personality or has something about them that would be distracting to the rest of the jury, I want to keep out. And of course, I'm looking to draw out any bias a juror might have that would keep them from following the law and coming to a decision based on the evidence instead of their personal preferences.

After the jury selection process is over, I move on to preparing what I'll say and do during the trial, starting with the police reports. I have to plan out the questions I will ask my witnesses so that I prove every element required. At that point, I'm set for the trial.

There are some things that develop as the trial goes on. You can only prepare so much for cross-examination, which is where the prosecutor gets to question the defense's witnesses. I didn't prepare for my cross-examinations in the same way, because it was more like shooting from the hip. I developed questions for them in the moment as I listened to the defense question them. It wasn't as rigid and controlled as when I examined my own witnesses.

The most important thing, when it comes to preparation and questioning for the actual trial, is to never ask a question that you don't know the answer to. I'd never put someone up on the stand without getting a feel for whether they were going to go sideways. You ask a question you don't know the answer to, or without having at least an idea of what they'll say, and you're likely to get burned.

> EVERY QUESTION I ASK IS LIKE SETTING UP A DOMINO FOR THE CLOSING ARGUMENT.

You also don't want to ask too many questions. You have to know when to stop pressing for details and look for the conclusion that you can work with later. Keep dabbling around and asking more, and you might end up proving the case for your opponent. Every question I ask is like setting up a domino for the closing argument. Each leads to what I want to say there. I don't want to tip over the domino early, so I have to know when to stop questioning.

PREP AS A DEFENSE ATTORNEY

As a defense attorney, I don't prepare for a case in exactly the same way as I did when I was a prosecutor, but it's still systematic so that it's thorough.

I start by looking at the evidence and the case closely, but instead of looking to see that every element is present to prove the charges, I'm looking for places where elements are not met, where something was missed. Those gaps are a good place to make my case.

I start looking at the evidence and what the DA has provided to see if there are holes in the evidence or in the amount of preparation. Poor preparation often means the other attorney is unfamiliar with their case, its strengths, or its weaknesses. Or maybe they're just not prepared to go to trial when push comes to shove. That's a dangerous game to play and one that I have to be prepared to capitalize on, as it will change the strength of the case. If a witness or officer comes in unprepared, I'm going to highlight that. After all, if they don't value the case enough to prepare, why should the jury value what they have to say?

I had a case where a witness to an assault didn't speak any English. I could hear on the recording that police were using a translator, and both the witness and the police officer acknowledged on the recording that they didn't understand each other's language. The final police report, however, didn't mention that the witness wasn't speaking English and that they used a translator.

The DA hadn't included any translators on their witness list. The police report didn't list it, and the DA didn't check the recording.

I found my angle. How do we know the translator on the recording, which was crucial to this case, was reliable? That was the question that opened the testimony up to doubt. I could wait for the DA to finish questioning the officer, then point out that the police used a translator, and take the questioning down that trail. If the DA wasn't prepared and relied only on the police report instead of listening to the actual recording, the entire witness statement could be thrown out and the case dismissed.

As the defense, I also have to put together the instructions I want to read to the jury, my witness list, and any proposed exhibits to be sent to the DA. I'll write a pretrial motion indicating what I want to keep out of the DA's case. I might address evidence gathered by an illegal search, for example, and ask that it be kept out.

Then I create questions for jury selection that cater to the outcome I want for the case. There are some similarities to the approach I took as a prosecutor. I want jurors who would be favorable to the case I plan on presenting. My preparation is based on what I'm advocating for.

BUILD YOUR OWN MODEL FOR PREPARATION

While every lawyer has to try a case within the same laws, not everyone prepares the same way.

Whether as a prosecutor or as a defense attorney, I created a model of preparation that I knew would serve me and my clients well. It's a mix of evaluation, paperwork, legal requirements, and sheer organization of many pieces into one solid case, starting with pretrial, jury selection, and what I'll actually do during the trial.

That's complex, and complexity is difficult. It's why I'm a big fan of checklists.

In 1935, what came to be known as the B-17 Flying Fortress crashed during a test flight just a few hundred feet after takeoff. There was nothing wrong with the airplane. The crash was due to pilot error. The new plane was much more complicated to operate than previous aircraft, and the crew had forgotten to remove a control lock for the elevator and rudder.

One mistake took the entire crew down.

The B-17 came close to being scrapped because it seemed impossible for pilots to master, but Boeing decided to do something different: create a checklist and organize the complexity.

From then on, checklists became the norm for aviation, all the way up to the space program. They were so important to the Apollo missions that Apollo 11 astronaut Michael Collins referred to them as the "fourth crew member." The medical industry even adopted the approach after seeing how checklists changed aviation.

Being prepared when faced with a complex scenario, like a criminal case with lots of witnesses and angles of attack, can be overwhelming without a checklist. You need a tool that helps you organize and break a problem down into smaller portions that you can prepare for.

You have to create your own checklist based on what you want your outcome to be. Pilots use detailed checklists before flights, setting up for takeoff, during the flight when at cruising altitude, and when landing and taxiing. There's a checklist for every aspect of normal flight. And all those checklists mean more time is tagged onto the pre- and post-flight.

Why so much fuss? Wouldn't it be easier to hop in the plane and go?

It would, but because their ultimate goal is to not crash the plane or lose their license, they put in the extra preparation that checklists require.

Because they want to get from point A to point B safely, pilots have checklists not just for normal flight, but also for the situations that might pop up along the way. There's a checklist for when your engine fails. A checklist for when you find yourself in icing conditions. A checklist for when you stall. A checklist for when you find yourself in IFR (instrument flight rules) conditions on a VFR (visual flight rules) flight. When your goal is to get to a destination safely, you have to prepare for both the known and unknown possible scenarios that might stop you along the way.

As a criminal defense attorney, I do the same.

My pretrial preparation is like that pilot's preflight checklist. Like the pilot is looking for anything that could end the flight, I'm looking for anything that could destroy my case. My general checklist looks like this:

1. Review charges.
2. Be aware of elements needed to prove each charge and any possible defenses to those charges.
3. Read police reports for evaluation and understanding.
4. Review evidence.
5. Reread police reports and reexamine evidence to determine what defenses are available, then select the best defense.
6. Take any steps necessary to put on best defense (for example, further investigation).

I use this master checklist for my overall preparation for a case, and I have checklists within each step. They might not all be as formalized as a pilot would have, but they are habitual. These are checklists that fit the specific situation and prepare for both the known and the potential unknown. I follow the process every time because I know if I do, I won't have to worry about a missed control lock bringing my case down.

The mere act of creating a checklist has some benefits. You're forced to identify real and potential problems. Preparation is impossible if you don't understand what problems need solving. One way I identify problems is to use four questions that dissect complexity:

PREPARATION IS IMPOSSIBLE IF YOU DON'T UNDERSTAND WHAT PROBLEMS NEED SOLVING.

1. What's my ultimate goal?
2. What do I need to make that happen?
3. What do I already have?
4. What's my approach going to be?

The fourth question is a heavy one because your approach is going to change based on your *understanding* of the problem. Situations change as you get new information, and when situations change, how you prepare to handle them changes too. Your skill at handling a fluid problem is only as flexible as how well you've evaluated it, thought it through, and prepared for the variables. But all those steps won't help you if you don't understand the situation as a whole.

CLOSING REMARKS

Luck is a gamble, whereas preparation and patience are an investment. I never want to hang the outcome of my case on a gamble. I would much rather invest in the outcome with patience and preparation than leave it to chance.

When you're prepared for a situation, you have more control. Surprises will still pop up, but you will be better able to handle them. Remember, the more prepared person is always going to take control of a situation. They can outperform someone who is smart or naturally gifted but underprepared.

Preparation is about going that extra mile. Prepare beyond what you think you'll ever need.

Great preparation uses a system, like checklists, to make sure you avoid gaps in your preparation. It means identifying the players in the situation and what they want. It confronts complexity by revisiting where you want to go, how you'll get there, and what you have in your possession. What's left unanswered is where you need to prepare.

Preparation is the hard work that lays the groundwork for everything that leads to winning.

CHAPTER 5:
UNDERSTANDING

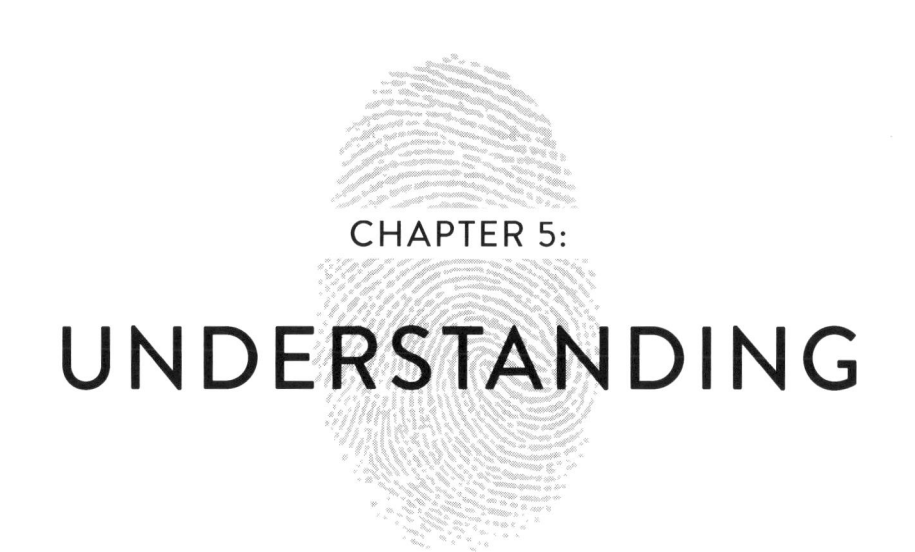

"Show them the drugs," I told the deputy.

This was a critical moment in the case I was prosecuting. I just didn't know how critical at the time, though I was about to find out.

A guy had been picked up with a ridiculous amount of meth and tried to lie his way to lesser charges. Anyone who is caught with illegal drugs and has any familiarity with the system uses the same defense: denial. Either they're not their drugs or, if that's too much of a reach to believe, they at least deny the intent to sell them. This guy was taking the second route.

"I was having a little get-together," he said. "I just wanted some for the party."

It must've been some party because there were over a thousand doses.

I was pretty sure I had an open-and-shut case for possession with intent to sell. I had a deputy involved with the case, who was experienced with drug cases, testify about what that amount really meant in terms of whether it could possibly be for personal use.

"If I buy a bushel of bananas, it's for personal use. If I buy a truckload, it's for sales," the deputy said. The jury was clearly convinced by his testimony.

But then I got the idea to build on that testimony to go for the home run. I thought it would be good to help the jury understand exactly what we were talking about in visual terms instead of just tossing numbers around. That amount of drugs was significant, and even my colleagues encouraged me to bring in the actual physical evidence.

"Don't just bring in a photo," they said. "Bring in the actual drugs. Show the jury. It'll make it more real, and they can get a sense of what it actually looks like."

I decided to run with it, even though my approach has always been to keep things simple. Once you start bringing in physical evidence, it's another variable; you have to properly manage how you handle it, and you introduce the potential for more things to go wrong. But this seemed like a slam dunk case, and the amount of drugs was so much that I figured the jury would like to see it. So I asked the deputy to bring the evidence bag with the drugs.

"Check the drugs out from evidence and bring them into court," I told him. "I'll ask you about them, and then I want you to show them to the jury."

Smooth sailing, it seemed. The deputy showed up with the brown paper bag from evidence with him the next day at court.

"Are those the drugs?" I asked him.

"Yes," he said.

"You got those from evidence?"

"Yes."

"You looked at them?"

"Yes."

Soon the deputy was back up on the stand, and I went over the case with him again, the jury listening as he described how they caught the guy with the drugs. I had him go over the importance of the amount of drugs, and then I pointed to the brown evidence bag. "Are those the drugs?"

"Yes," he said.

"Show them the drugs," I said.

He cut the tape on the bag and opened it up, verifying it again as the drugs he found. I went ahead with my questioning and left the bag on the table for the jury to see.

The defense attorney got up next to start her questioning, briefly looking at the bag of drugs on the table. She paused, and then began frantically looking through her notes.

When you plan a big, showy moment, you'd better understand what you're doing. If you don't, your big moment could turn out to be just what the opposition needs to get the win. The defense attorney began her questioning, asking the deputy to pick up the bag of drugs.

"Can you point to the defendant's name on the evidence bag?" she asked him.

"Of course," he said, picking up the bag. "It's right here . . ." His voice faded, and he paused for a moment. "Um, I don't see it."

"What do you mean you don't see it?"

"There's actually someone else's name on here," he said with a panicked voice.

Oh, shit. This wasn't what I'd planned.

The deputy looked at me like a deer in headlights, as if I were a wizard who could magically fix the huge mess he'd just created. I shook my head in disbelief. The defense attorney grilled him for the rest of the morning until the lunch break. There was nothing I could do but watch.

All of this in front of the jury.

As it turns out, the evidence room clerk had grabbed the wrong bag for a completely different case because they were of a similar amount of drugs. The deputy never checked the name on it. And from that point, I knew this was going to be an incredibly difficult case. The deputy's credibility was destroyed. He had made a massive mistake, going from an asset to a liability when he looked lost and confused on the stand.

Ultimately, the jury only found the defendant guilty of possession and *not* intent to sell. And it was simply because they lost confidence in the deputy. It went from a felony with lots of consequences to a misdemeanor with very few, all because of a mistake and a misunderstanding. Had the defendant not taken the stand at all, he may not have been convicted of anything. They came back with a verdict that aligned with who they thought had more credibility. Unfortunately for me, because of the officer's mistake, the defendant won that race.

It's not the outcome I would've liked. But I do see how they got there, and I can't fault them for the decision. I misunderstood the monumental importance of the situation, and the decisions I made based on that misunderstanding hurt my case.

MISUNDERSTANDING WILL COST YOU BIG

There are no simple misunderstandings.

When you make a mistake, you have to own it, and in that drug case, I made a mistake. I didn't understand how crucial that moment was, or what potential consequences there would be, until it was too late. I should have made sure I completely understood the situation before I got to that *oh shit* moment.

Having the wrong bag of drugs brought in was the obvious error, but so was deciding to bring in evidence to make the case more "sexy" without considering whether it was necessary or if it could backfire. The jury appeared to believe the deputy's testimony, and the evidence was clear that the defendant had the drugs on him; but I still went ahead to provide them with a visual experience anyway.

> THE MORE VARIABLES YOU INTRODUCE, THE MORE POTENTIAL FOR THINGS TO GO WRONG.

When I made the decision to introduce the drugs, the case was going well. The jury had no reason to question the deputy's credibility. I introduced a new piece of evidence—but for what? It was unlikely I needed it to win the case. The more variables you introduce, the more potential for things to go wrong. As in so many things, less is often more.

Each situation we find ourselves in is like the human body, with distinct systems that are dependent or operate in unison with other systems. I can evaluate each system on its own, but that won't necessarily help me understand how they work together. Or maybe it helps to think of our decisions like tossing a rock into a pond. There's the moment of impact, which is hopefully what we're expecting, but there are also ripples that spread out from there. You have to understand where the ripples might go.

The evaluation process we talked about in the last chapter is what leads to understanding. It's the culmination of everything you've been working up to, your final read on a situation.

And when you understand things, you can use them to your advantage.

UNDERSTAND HOW RULES APPLY TO THE SITUATION

Imagine the worst episode of the reality show *Hoarders*, set inside a run-down shed behind a house desperately in need of some new paint. In this setting, weeds sprouted on the edge of the driveway where four cars were parked, and they ran along the edge of the fence and the base of the buildings, making the old shed appear unused.

Yet the police were interested in the shed.

Boxes and containers were packed in at every angle, filling shelves that sagged under the weight. It was difficult to find a clear path through the mess, much less find anything at all. For the police to find a small gun tucked at the bottom of a tin container was nothing short of a miracle.

The chaos of the shed would make my job of prosecuting the defendant really tough.

As a felon, he wasn't allowed to possess a weapon. But could I really prove that the gun buried in the bottom of that mess was actually his? It'd be easy for the defense to claim that some of that collection of junk, including the gun, was the property of one of the other people who called that run-down house *home*.

For a successful conviction, I had to show the defendant knowingly possessed that gun. During interviews, he didn't indicate any knowledge of the gun, and it was clear I had to figure out a way to get that proof.

Getting that proof meant I had to understand how people thought and acted, and how the rules applied. I knew that jail phone calls were recorded. And I knew he was still in jail.

"Go down to the jail and pull his calls," I told my investigator. "I want to know who he's talking to and what he's saying."

Keep in mind that the guy had been in jail for almost a year. There were hundreds of phone calls to go through, and I didn't have the time to review all of them. I had to figure out a more manageable way to approach

UNDERSTANDING THE RULES ISN'T ENOUGH; YOU HAVE TO UNDERSTAND HOW TO APPLY THEM TO THE SITUATION.

the recordings, so I decided to look at the jail calls around his court dates. Understanding human nature, I figured he'd be most likely to talk freely to his people about what had just happened in court.

A few calls in, I hit the jackpot.

"How'd your court case go?" I heard a raspy voice ask.

The defendant cleared his throat and mumbled that it went OK.

"What did they get you for again?"

"They found my gun," he replied. "They found my damn gun in that container I hid it in, in the shed."

I heard the other voice curse, and the defendant continued. "I hid it so good I forgot it was there until those damn cops come up to me and say 'what's this?'" He paused, and then laughed. "I didn't tell them a thing though, so they ain't got nothin' on me. They can't prove that it's my gun. Five other people in that damn house. It could be anybody's for all those cops know."

Thank you, thank you, thank you.

The defendant was right. He knew exactly where the weakness was in my case. He just didn't understand how he was helping me fill that gap. Before you even talk on the phone while in jail, they tell you it's recorded. But these guys still spill the beans anyway. They don't take it seriously, and they're willing to say things they shouldn't. In contrast, I understood that they do this all the time.

Understanding the rules isn't enough; you have to understand how to apply them to the situation. And to win, you have to understand that application better than your opponent. One case in particular comes to mind.

Two guys walked into a bar, and no, this is not the start of a joke.

One of them, a scruffy, hot-tempered man who looked like he hadn't eaten in months, started harassing and egging on another man sitting at the bar. Words went to fists, and fists went to face, with the scruffy fellow taking the first swing. Not only did he pick a fight with the wrong guy and got a pounding in return, but he also faced charges for starting the fight.

To an outside observer, like the jury, it would seem like a large barroom bully beat up a weaker man. I had a strong suspicion, despite the facts of the case, that the defendant's attorney would claim self-defense. From first glance, it would seem like a solid win. If you're acting in self-defense, it's not assault.

Except I understood a couple of things about the rules of self-defense.

I knew what was needed to prove self-defense, and I also knew you couldn't use it as a defense unless evidence was introduced that showed it was credible. For example, no matter how you feel about mimes, you can't just go up to a street performer and punch him in the face three times and then claim self-defense. There has to be sufficient evidence that you were defending yourself from harm. Without that introduced in trial, you can't argue self-defense.

In court, I called my witness, the seemingly larger barroom bully. From experience and conversations with the defense attorney where I observed that her client had an anger problem, I knew what she was going to try. When it was her turn to question my witness, she asked him to describe what happened.

"He took a swing at me," my witness said. "I swung back."

That's all she could get out of him. He never once changed his testimony. And since the defense attorney knew her client had a short fuse, she didn't call him to the stand to give me a chance to push his buttons and get him to show the jury his anger. The only evidence presented during the trial was what my witness said.

When it came time to instruct the jury, the defense attorney requested that the judge read the self-defense instructions to the jury.

I spoke up. "We don't have any evidence of self-defense in this case."

"What do you mean we don't have any evidence? My guy got beat up. He was hurt pretty badly," she said.

And this is where I knew I had her. The rules say you have to present sufficient evidence of self-defense before you can have a reading of the self-defense instructions to the jury. She hadn't done that since she hadn't allowed her client to testify on the stand.

"The only testimony we have in this case is that the defendant swung first," I said. "There was no other witness testimony or evidence otherwise."

She was backed into the corner without the ability to argue self-defense. She knew some of the rules, but she hadn't bothered to look at the footnotes. Because of that, she didn't fully understand the situation she was in.

The key to understanding is that just knowing the rules isn't enough. You have to know how to use them. It's about true situational awareness because true understanding rests on seeing the full situation.

Of course, the only constant is that things change, which means that understanding is fluid and always shifting. When the situation you thought you understood changes, you have to be willing to change your understanding. Variables shift, something in the complex system is altered, everything changes, and you have to reevaluate what you thought you knew. The rules you thought applied yesterday might not apply today.

For example, imagine a situation in which someone who doesn't want to miss their exit cuts off another driver by merging across a few lanes on the freeway. A pursuit ensues, and the two cars end up at a gas station where the road rage turns into an assault. Trying that case should be an easy win, right? No jury would be OK with that kind of behavior.

But what if the driver who did that last-minute merge had a bumper sticker for some group or organization that was controversial? Suddenly, the jury might think such a person would deserve an assault. I'd better have an understanding of the situation, of current events or cultural shifts, and what rules apply, instead of operating on assumptions.

> THE KEY TO UNDERSTANDING IS THAT JUST KNOWING THE RULES ISN'T ENOUGH. YOU HAVE TO KNOW HOW TO USE THEM.

UNDERSTAND THE PLAYERS

I don't assume every attorney I come up against hasn't fully read the footnotes for every legal rule that applies to the case. Each player in the game is different.

With the self-defense case, simple observation of both the attorney and the client told me how they would likely handle it.

I saw her client get angry and yell, and I knew she wouldn't put him on the stand. I also knew that self-defense was the most likely defense to take, not just from experience, but from things she'd said to me in conversations. Knowing her client wasn't going to testify and that there were no other witnesses listed told me she hadn't paid attention to the bench notes, so I was ready with my highlighted copy of the jury instructions. Once I heard her opening statement, I knew I understood the situation correctly.

First, you have to know what game you're playing. That means you understand the rules of the game, who the players are, and how those players might respond during the game. The game is fluid, and so are the players. Who are the decision-makers? Who are the influencers? Who are the enemies? Who are the allies? What are their respective roles in the game? Once you know their roles and how those roles define or limit what they'll do, you will know how to evaluate every piece of information, both intentional and unintentional, they give you.

You also have to understand what they want, why they're doing what they're doing, and how they'll most likely get there. The reason for people's actions is often more important than the action itself. Actions don't spontaneously happen; they stem from some kind of motivation that can give you a heads-up on predicting their behavior.

Baby rattlesnakes are a good example of this.

Full-grown rattlesnakes are venomous, and they look terrifying. But the baby rattlesnake is what you really have to watch out for. They're young and haven't learned to regulate the amount of venom they use when they bite. Their bite is incredibly venomous because they're inexperienced. They don't understand how much force is needed to take down an adversary. Everyone who crosses their path will get the full force of the bite, no matter the situation.

When we first start something, we're almost always excited about it. New job, first day of school—what's new is exciting, and it's the same thing for attorneys. You've gone through undergrad, law school, the bar exam, and all kinds of other hellish requirements—and finally, here you are. You're ready to make a difference. You're itching to jump in.

But you have no experience.

You have knowledge, but no experience. You have no idea how to turn that knowledge into understanding. You don't know how to interact with people or how to negotiate a case. You're missing the practical skills. You have to learn, or you'll fail.

Maybe in your enthusiasm, you think you'll prosecute every case, big or small, without realizing what a bad idea that is. You have no clue you'll burn yourself out, ruin your credibility, and create a personal identity crisis where you'll end up questioning your skills.

On an extremely hot day, a homeless woman had gone into a convenience store and filled up a small cup with ice and soda. You can't blame her; the heat was visibly radiating off of the asphalt. She walked out of the store without paying and technically stole $1.50 worth of soda.

A brand new DA was eager to prosecute because new DAs want to prosecute everything.

Sure, technically it was theft. But are you going to get a jury who's willing to convict for such a thing? Does the store even want you to prosecute? Is it even an appropriate use of your skills and the cost of the trial? The question isn't always if you can prove a case, but if you should.

This goes back to understanding.

Watching new DAs aggressively pursuing cases that weren't worth it was like watching someone use a samurai sword to cut a thread. They enlisted investigators and subpoenas and the full strength of the law on things like $1.50 sodas or public drunkenness.

They were like those baby rattlesnakes. Their actions make sense when you understand the motivation behind them.

It's easy to get caught up in what a person is doing, but that's a short-lived observation that only serves you in that moment. If you can figure out *why* someone is doing what they're doing, you can predict or at least make an educated guess on *what* they'll do next.

Whenever new DAs behaved like baby rattlesnakes, they'd set themselves up for failure. What happens when they lose the Great Soda Heist case not because of skill, but because they shouldn't have tried it in the first place? They lose confidence.

As a defense attorney, I recognize this kind of behavior, and I know what motivates them to do this. I can use this to understand how to try my case because understanding how people respond means I have lots of options on how to relate to those people.

Observe. Evaluate. Spot patterns. Look for moments when someone makes a decision that locks them into a path they can't go back from. Capitalize on that moment.

UNDERSTAND YOUR VULNERABILITIES

Always be looking for cracks in the wall, including your own.

Take burglary, for example. The definition of burglary is the entry of a building or property with the intent to commit felony or theft. That is, before you go in, you have to have the intention of stealing. You can't form intent after you get inside.

As a prosecutor, the issue of intent is my crack in the wall. I need to shore it up and prove intent. I might look to see if the person had any money on them as proof that they intended to buy something. Going into a store without any means of payment might help prove intent. Or, if the person is caught on video walking very directly to the electronics, pocketing an item, and immediately leaving, their actions indicate an apparent intent to go in, take something, and leave.

Good prosecutors are going to look at a case and figure out where a defense attorney will likely attack. Good defense attorneys look at the same case and pick the element that will be most difficult to prove. You have to understand the strategy of each player's roles. If you're playing prosecution, you can't let any players through. But if you're playing defense, you only need to get one through.

Prosecutors have the burden, which makes them oddly defensive. They have a castle with four walls, and they can't let anything in. The defense attorney, on the other hand, is on the offensive. They have to get at least one person through the walls at any cost. But here's the trick: they don't have to attack all four walls. One small corner, with a little crack to get started, will do just fine.

Every person has vulnerabilities.

My great uncle fought in World War II, and he would describe how fierce the tanks looked as they came toward you. Gun turrets, armored plating—impossible to fight. That was, until they moved past you and you saw the backside. There you could see the engine, and all the guns were pointing in the other direction. There wasn't as much armor plating on the back as the front. Just like the Death Star, everything has a weakness, no matter how impenetrable it may seem.

Understanding the vulnerabilities of people is part of understanding the players.

If you want to strengthen your own position, look for insecurities. Figure out all possible angles. Find the weaknesses. Set a trap to make a strength seem like a weakness.

Because they're doing this to you too.

UNDERSTANDING IN EVERYDAY LIFE

Much of our life we live on autopilot. Our habits and assumptions make it possible to not have to think about every decision we make every moment of the day.

That's not bad. It keeps us from paralyzing moments where we can't decide if we should eat breakfast or not; we have the habit, so we don't have to think about it. We can save our energy for more important decisions. But too much autopilot gets in the way of understanding important things because it assumes things never change.

When I get up in the morning and see the sun shining brightly, I know from past experience that the weather can change later in the day. Looking at the weather report might cause me to prepare for a rainy afternoon despite the sun right now. I also know it might be cooler in the morning, but it'll be hot by 2 p.m.

Circumstances change. Information changes. Continued exposure is continued revelation. That means that understanding is a fluid thing, not static. It requires you to be willing to change because decisions are driven by new understanding. This is why constant evaluation, as we discussed earlier in chapter 2, is essential.

What you understood yesterday might be different today. What you understood five minutes ago might have just changed. We easily grasp this when it comes to something obvious like the weather, but don't always put it into practice in other areas of life. Most of us run by making decisions off of information that has gone way past its shelf life. You have to keep your information fresh if you want your understanding to stay fluid and up-to-date.

WHAT YOU UNDERSTOOD YESTERDAY MIGHT BE DIFFERENT TODAY. WHAT YOU UNDERSTOOD FIVE MINUTES AGO MIGHT HAVE JUST CHANGED.

As an attorney, it's important that I understand what the witness is telling me. I have to use that to build my defense. That means I ask a lot of open-ended questions to get the best information for what I'm trying to prove.

"Tell me about the day."

"Tell me what happened."

"What were you feeling?"

"What were you doing?"

"What did you see?"

Building understanding for the jury is about setting the stage, and open questions are a good way to do that.

Leading questions are different. They lead a witness to where you want them to go and are a good way, during cross-examination, to prove a point or show that a witness isn't being honest.

But you can't lead if you don't know where you're leading to. That's why both open and leading questions are viable tools. Open-ended questions build a foundation of information where the responses don't matter. They are fact-finding questions for your understanding. When the answer matters to your case, though, leading questions are the way to go. They are questions for the jury's understanding.

> AND AS ALL LAWYERS KNOW, WORDS MATTER.

What is your goal in questioning?

You have to know what you want from your questions because how you frame them is what you get back. And as all lawyers know, words matter. Lawyers are wordsmiths.

"Officer, where did you see that person shoot?" a lawyer might ask in trial.

"I saw them shoot at the vehicle" is different from "I saw them shoot in the direction of the vehicle." One indicates purpose and intent. The other indicates the general geography of a gunshot.

One client of mine had shared an apartment with several other people. When police searched the apartment and found some stolen items, they accused my client of the theft.

"We want to talk about the stolen items in your apartment," the police asked my client. "Do you use that stolen TV?"

"Yeah, I watch it sometimes," my client responded.

The police asked a few other questions and never pressed my client more about the TV. But when they wrote up the report, they noted that my client admitted he was in possession of a stolen TV. It appeared, from the report, that he'd admitted to stealing the TV.

He didn't say that, exactly.

When I went back and listened to the recorded interview between my client and police, it was clear he never said he stole the TV. He acknowledged its presence and that he sometimes watched it, but he never outright said he stole it or even knew where it had come from.

During the trial, when the officer got up to testify that my client had stolen the TV and referred to the police report, I played the recorded interview so the jury could hear exactly what was said.

"Did my client actually say the TV was his?"

"Well yeah, he said he uses it . . ."

"OK, but did he say that the TV was his?"

"No, but it's in his apartment, and he said he watches it."

"But did my client actually say the TV was his?"

"Well, no."

"Did you come to that conclusion on your own?"

"Yes . . ."

Instead of trying to get more context, the officer had his eye on a quick conviction. Get an admission out of my client, and we would be good to go.

It would've been easy for him to ask a few follow-up questions. He could've asked my client if everything in the room was his or who had access to the room. Had he done that, he would've had my client admitting that everything in the room, including the TV, belonged to him. Or he could've asked where my client got the TV and followed that line of questioning to either the truth or an awkward, provable lie.

But he didn't ask any of those questions, which would have given him a solid report that would have been difficult to defend against. Instead, a sloppy investigation meant the officer built reasonable doubt into his case. If you take shortcuts, it has the potential to blow up in your face. Instead of trying to find out if there was a crime or not, he was looking for a suspect so he could move on.

Questions can force answers and cause people to come to false conclusions. People who have preconceived ideas will use this approach to manipulate people. It happens all the time in everyday life, whether it's in advertisements trying to sell you something or actual conversations. Understanding comes when you can identify that this is going on because understanding should lead to clarity, not confusion.

An indication that you understand something is that you can teach or explain it clearly to someone else. If you aren't clear about something, the person trying to give you information probably doesn't understand it well themselves or may be misleading you.

Here's a good litmus test to use if you think the information you're getting from someone is off: ask yourself questions.

1. Does this make sense?
2. Is it based on assumptions?
3. Are the questions leading me to a predetermined conclusion?
4. Does it leave me with a nagging sense of confusion or that something's not quite right?

One of the best ways to cut through this kind of fog is by using counterfactuals, which are questions that consider what didn't happen: What would have happened if the Allies hadn't won World War II? If Julius Caesar hadn't been assassinated? If we hadn't landed on the moon? If I didn't assume that guy was telling the truth?

When you understand, you can make solid decisions no matter the situation. You can come up with appropriate solutions to problems. Your results aren't based on guesswork.

Understanding isn't the end of it, though. It helps you make decisions, but decisions without action don't really take you anywhere. Understanding should lead you to preparation. I understood the defense attorney hadn't paid attention to the footnotes, but I had to prepare to present that to the judge to block her defense.

It's like taking a trip. You look at a map and figure out possible routes, evaluating for the best one. You evaluate what you'll need during the trip, like bathroom breaks or stopping for gas. And you'll do that because you're motivated to not be stranded along the side of the road, peeing behind a sage bush while big rigs roar by honking their horns.

Understanding without preparation and action takes you nowhere, and we are definitely headed somewhere.

CLOSING REMARKS

If you don't understand the room, you can't read the room.

Understanding is about recognizing there's a *whole* while also understanding the parts that make it up. Every situation has context that is made of people with different roles, cultures, emotions, and motivations. Your own strengths and weaknesses, which are now part of the situation, also play a part.

I remember visiting the Grand Canyon with my in-laws. It was their first time to stand on its rim and stare hundreds of feet into the earth. Being brought to tears on the edge of the Grand Canyon is certainly different than seeing a picture. You don't truly understand its grandeur until you've experienced it firsthand.

True understanding is not just about knowing all the rules or facts, but also:

1. Knowing how to rightly apply the rules in each situation
2. Knowing that situations can change over time and as new information is added
3. Being willing to rethink previous conclusions
4. Never running on assumptions, but seeing every situation as if it were new, no matter how familiar it might be

Perfect understanding might not be possible, but you can understand what's in your view and in your control, and you can use that to your advantage.

CHAPTER 6:

PERSUADING

The two bodies were sprawled across the ground, their glassy, unseeing eyes staring into the night.

The woman and the man lay on the narrow walkway that stretched between the front door and the yard gate. She'd been stabbed twelve times, with one wound gashing into her neck so deep it nearly severed it. The man lay nearby, with twenty stab wounds peppering his body, the woman's eyeglasses still in his hands. He'd only stopped by to return them when he interrupted the attack on the woman.

The entire scene was one of extreme brutality and force, the product of real rage. Blood was splattered across the bodies and the sidewalk, coagulating by the time police arrived. The woman's two children were asleep in the house the entire time and had heard nothing.

Police went to her ex-husband's house to let him know of her murder. When they arrived, the ex-husband was nowhere to be found, but they noticed blood smears on his vehicle and a bloody glove on the property. They had no idea how important that glove would be.

Because if the glove doesn't fit, you must acquit.

Whether that's true or not doesn't matter. If we're going to talk about the art of persuasion, we have to talk about the O. J. Simpson case.

The defense faced an unimaginable mountain of hard evidence that they had to overcome. They weren't under any illusion about the fight ahead of them.

The prosecution had so much evidence that pointed to O. J. being present at the scene that they thought they couldn't lose. It seemed like one of those slam dunk cases where the trial practically runs itself. They couldn't lose.

O. J. Simpson was acquitted.

Maybe the prosecution didn't explain the DNA evidence well enough that the jury could understand what was then a new type of evidence, long before the TV show *CSI* made it common knowledge. Maybe it was a bumbling of how the evidence was handled, how things weren't entered correctly into the chain of custody.

Or maybe they lost because the defense was better at persuading the jury. They were able to capitalize on every mistake that the prosecution made; nothing escaped their notice.

Remember how I told you that you should never ask a question that you don't know the answer to? Don't ask someone to put on a glove if you aren't sure the glove will fit. Don't rest an important visual moment of your case on something you haven't tested out.

The defense capitalized on that moment and came up with a catchy phrase—one that's still part of cultural memory today—that helped lock the jury's minds onto a path toward acquittal. It only took three hours for the jury to come back with a not guilty verdict.

Not only did the defense capitalize on that huge blunder made by the prosecution, but they persuasively wove it into the theme of the case they were making. The evidence, you see, was all planted by a dirty, racist cop.

Of course the glove won't fit, because it's planted.

Of course you'll find blood at the scene, because it's planted.

Of course the gloves were planted, because no self-respecting murderer drops a glove at the crime scene and then drops another back at his home.

Maybe it was all a coincidence. But the defense figured out that if you wove the right themes into your story, you could discredit an entire investigation by discrediting an investigator. You've provided a reason for why the evidence exists but can be ignored.

That's the chink in the armor, discrediting the investigator. That's the way to put a wedge into the prosecutor's case. It was no longer a case about a man brutally murdering his ex-wife and a bystander. It was now a sad case about an innocent man who was disliked and targeted by a corrupt and racist investigator.

Was it true?

It didn't matter.

The defense made enough of a persuasive argument that the jury couldn't be comfortable voting guilty. When it came time to decide, they couldn't be sure if Simpson was guilty beyond reasonable doubt. The defense had done just enough to call into question whether he did it, pointing to all the evidence with a reasonable explanation as to why he hadn't committed the crime.

At the start of the trial, no one would have thought it was reasonable to argue that it was a setup by the police. Nobody would have believed it. There was no motive for them to have done that. But suddenly a crucial piece of evidence pops up, and you figure out how to creatively weave that into a theme that will ultimately introduce reasonable doubt.

**WAS IT TRUE?
IT DIDN'T MATTER.**

Even better? If more evidence rolls in, it's easily added to your story. You're building on what you already started. You don't have to work so hard at persuading, because the ball is already rolling.

PERSUASION IS KNOWING WHAT PEOPLE WANT

Persuasion capitalizes on desire.

You can't create desire, because it either exists in a person or it doesn't. But persuasion can stoke that existing desire and direct (or redirect) it toward your end goal. To persuade someone, your job isn't to create a new desire; it's to find the one that already exists and build the connections between that and where you want them to go. You're leveraging that desire.

In a trial, persuasion starts early on, long before I get up to argue and question. It starts with picking the jury. If I pick the wrong jury,

PERSUASION IS AN ART THAT REQUIRES THE ABILITY TO RELATE TO PEOPLE, LEVERAGE THEIR DESIRE, AND BRING THEM TO YOUR CONCLUSION.

one unwilling to consider the verdict I want, my best persuasion will fail because nothing I do will move the needle. They have to want to consider the evidence and the possibility of either verdict. I have to get rid of anyone I think won't have an open mind.

Think of the pointless political arguments you've had online. It doesn't matter how much evidence you present and how good you are at persuading, some people simply refuse to be moved. They will not listen, and they will not be persuaded. They have no desire to change their mind.

Persuasion is an art that requires the ability to relate to people, leverage their desire, and bring them to your conclusion. It's about getting someone to move from one position to another. It's not about winning arguments but about winning hearts and minds.

If there's no desire, persuasion doesn't work.

THE GUY WITH THE SMOKING GUN

Remember the scene in the film *Big Daddy* with Adam Sandler where he's trying to order breakfast in a McDonald's? Adam Sandler plays Sonny Koufax, a lazy guy who adopts a five-year-old boy to impress his former girlfriend. In that scene at McDonald's, everything falls apart. First, the little boy wants lasagna. Second, they're too late to order breakfast. Third, a random guy scolds Sonny for his terrible parenting, and Sonny responds by dumping out the man's french fries. Everyone in the place turns against him, and the kid is wailing. Sonny finally loses it and yells: "Will somebody get the kid a Happy Meal?!"

That scene at McDonald's is a bit like a case I had as a prosecutor.

While waiting in line at a busy fast food restaurant over the lunch hour, a man in his fifties cut ahead of several people, announcing he had to get back to work before his lunch hour was over. There was some grumbling because a lot of people at fast food restaurants are in a hurry, but a younger guy was noticeably angry about this turn of events. And it was more than mere grumbling.

The two got into an argument, causing the restaurant to clear out a bit as people decided to walk away and try the drive-through instead of getting involved in a lobby brawl. The older man got his food and then went outside and hopped into his car. Instead of sticking around to order anything, the younger guy got in his car and followed the man.

He followed for over four miles to where the older man worked, pulling in behind him in the parking lot of his office. The older man was alarmed and tried to get out of the car and into the office building with his lunch as quickly as he could. He didn't make it. The angry driver got out of his car, easily a foot taller than the older man, looking like he could be an NFL linebacker, as angry as he was big. He ran up and swung a massive fist at the older guy's face; his nose didn't stand a chance. The older guy crumpled to the ground. And then a bystander yelled, "He's got a gun!" The incident ended with the attacker threatening the older man for good measure.

I figured this wouldn't be difficult to prosecute.

This is the kind of scenario that terrifies people, where an otherwise normal encounter is someone's last straw, causing them to snap and go after you. It had all the pieces of assault, criminal threats, and brandishing a weapon. I figured a jury should be very receptive to convicting someone who would behave like this. Even better, there were witnesses to the entire event. Should have been an easy win.

One of the witnesses said the defendant's car was still running, driver side door open, parked at an angle. There was screaming and yelling. The defendant grabbed the fast food bag from the victim and threw it to the ground, stomping on it. There were obscenities. Lots of obscenities. The defendant swung his fist into the victim's face, which made a distinct popping sound. When the defendant reached for his waist, the witness wasn't going to wait to find out what he was going to grab. He immediately ducked behind a big trash can, but he did remember hearing someone else yell, "He's got a gun!" But unfortunately, none of the other witnesses interviewed saw a gun, meaning whoever yelled about the gun didn't stick around the scene.

Despite not being able to see a gun, the witness could clearly hear the defendant say, "Consider yourself lucky, bitch. If you ever piss me off again, you'll be even sorrier." After that, the defendant could be seen running back to his car. Hearing the defendant get back into his car, the witness peeked around the trash can and saw him speed away.

The photos of the aftermath were powerful. The victim's nose was severely bent out of shape, clearly broken, and there was blood all over his face.

It was amazing evidence. The case practically presented itself.

If the guy lands a hit, you can't acquit, right?

The only tricky part was the gun. The victim testified at trial that he'd heard someone yell, "He's got a gun!" But he couldn't actually see it, because he'd just gotten his nose broken. Add to that, another bystander told police that they didn't see a gun but definitely thought the attacker was reaching for a weapon of some sort. To cap it all off, when the police finally apprehended the defendant, he (obviously) didn't have a gun in his possession. In fact, he wasn't even a registered gun owner. There were witnesses, but they didn't see any gun either. They saw the defendant reaching for something, and my client said it was a gun because he heard someone yell "He's got a gun," but without any proof, it was my client's word against his attacker's.

As it turns out, you can get sympathy for just about anyone if you weave the right story. Just like the O. J. Simpson case, the defense had a story to weave. If they could change the way the jury felt about the victim, the defense could also change the way they felt about the defendant.

In this specific case, the defense wanted to make the jury aware of the victim's criminal history. They wanted to provide the disgusting details of a past crime involving kids, details no one wanted to hear about. The goal of this was to persuade the jury that they couldn't trust anything the victim said or did, because he had a criminal past. The defense wanted to sneak these past charges into the current case to demolish the victim's likability. Once a jury member forms an opinion on someone or something, it's an uphill battle to get them to change it.

This is a tactic lawyers use a lot. If you can slip in things like a criminal past into a current case, it can be very damaging. It reframes the situation for the jury. It's a natural human response to react emotionally to something like a criminal past involving kids, but sometimes when emotions take over, justice isn't done. As the prosecutor, my job was to make sure the law was followed and the person who did something wrong was held accountable for their actions.

"This past history isn't relevant to this case," I said to the judge, trying to keep the information out of the trial. "The defendant never knew the victim, so what he did in his past had no role in what happened."

No luck. The judge wasn't agreeing, so I tried again.

"I don't care if you tell them he's a convicted felon," I said. "That's fine. Tell them he has a criminal past if you have to, but the details don't matter in this case."

Nope. All the gory details were allowed in. So, instead of being a case about someone going off his rocker, beating up a random person, and possibly having an anger issue that could cause future problems, it became one about karma. The victim deserved it.

I tried to lessen the impact during jury selection to emphasize that even though someone had a past, they still deserved equal protection under the law. And then, once the trial started, I brought up my client's past before the defense could, trying to counteract it and set the direction for where I wanted the jury to go. But the defense still had a field day.

"Isn't it true that you're a convicted sex offender?"

"Isn't it true that you were convicted on two separate occasions for touching little children inappropriately?"

It was hard to hear those questions without being able to do anything. I looked over at the jury, and sure enough, the damage had been done. I knew it was going to be very hard to hold the defendant accountable now, but I still gave the case my all.

I presented the best closing argument I could to the jury:

"Everyone, regardless of their past, deserves to be protected by the law. No one deserves to be terrorized, assaulted, and injured the way this victim was, for no good reason other than someone else's road rage."

It didn't matter, though. The jury came back not guilty on all felony charges and convicted only on a misdemeanor simple battery. The video, after all, hadn't shown an actual gun. It suggested the presence of a gun but hadn't shown it. The defendant could've been reaching at his waistband to pull up his pants for all the jury knew.

Every juror understood the idea of equal protection, but there are some things people can't get past. The defense had no defense for the actual case, but because they understood the innate desire of people to condemn child molesters, they found the one thing that would blow a case out of the water. They capitalized on people's emotions.

Persuasion rises and falls on people's passions and emotions, and a jury of twelve people is a jury of twelve emotional beings.

Technically, I won the case. The defendant was convicted of a crime: simple battery. But given the severity of his conduct, a simple battery conviction wasn't much consolation.

What happened was serious felony assault. The defendant should have lost his right to own firearms because he had a known history of this kind of random rage toward people, either chasing them down or punching them. Unfortunately, that background was not let in by the judge. So the jury was left with an incomplete picture: one person with a disgusting past and another with seemingly no criminal history. You have to do the best with what you have.

PERSUASION IS FACTS WRAPPED IN EMOTION

We make a mistake when we think persuasion is about facts.

Facts have a role, but persuasion is mostly about leveraging emotion. It's the art of presenting the facts wrapped up in a story that leverages the desires and emotions already present. Presenting only facts in an effort to persuade is a lot of work, but if you can tap into a person's emotions, it only takes a tiny nudge to persuade.

Don't mistake me here; the art of persuasion isn't the art of lying. That's never acceptable. If you persuade people through lies, the boomerang you'll experience when the lies are uncovered is substantial.

In a trial, I want to make sure what I use to persuade is accurate. It would be unethical to mislead the jury or the court with lies and deception (but sadly, there are some attorneys out there for whom honesty takes a back seat to winning). There's a big difference between raising reasonable doubt and simply making something up. Almost always, the best defense is based in truth. A defense built on lies is a ticking time bomb that almost always goes off. And when it does, things get messy.

That's not always the case in the real world. Some individuals have found ways to use deception to their advantage when trying to persuade people.

> **FACTS HAVE A ROLE, BUT PERSUASION IS MOSTLY ABOUT LEVERAGING EMOTION.**

People have figured out that persuasion has some shortcuts. False equations are the most common. If you can find a way to associate a person or an idea with something emotionally distasteful, it doesn't take much to make people turn on the person or idea, whether it's justified by reality or not. You've persuaded them that the two are the same, and the disgust you feel for one should be felt for the other.

It's critical that you understand this because persuasion is being used on you all the time. There's rarely a moment where someone isn't trying to persuade you. If you're reading the news, there's persuasion. If you're seeing ads, there's persuasion. If you're watching a TV show, there's persuasion. If you're scrolling through social media, there's persuasion.

Someone wants you to buy, someone wants you to believe, someone wants you to reject. Someone wants to change the way you think about something. And they're using persuasion and your emotions to do it. Strong persuasion can get people to deny what they're seeing with their own eyes.

"Yes, that incredibly violent man punched a guy in the face, and yes, I have no doubt that's what happened because I can see it on the video, but disgusting people like that deserve it."

When you know how persuasion works, you're ahead of the game. The lawyer mindset can teach you to persuade and also protect you from persuasion.

PERSUADE ANYONE, USING A LAWYER'S MINDSET

When it comes to persuading people, there are a few things I rely on when I'm in the courtroom.

Understanding the emotional component is probably the biggest piece of the puzzle, but I also need to truly believe in what I'm persuading people to think. Unless you're a sociopath, you can't fake real belief when you're persuading people. If you believe what you're selling, then the goal is to telegraph your belief and be assertive about it.

What does that look like?

It's about physical presence and posture, your tone, and the language you use to present your argument.

Let's say you walk into an electronics store to buy a TV. A young saleswoman comes up to you and begins telling you about a model you're considering.

"They say this is the best TV you can get," she says, her hands in her pockets. She shuffles her feet a bit as she looks at the TV. "I'm told it has an amazing picture quality, and I understand you can turn it on using your voice. I think it's supposed to be very reliable."

Now let's try a different version.

"This is the best TV you can get," she says, looking you in the eye. She moves over to the TV and points to the screen while looking back at you. "It has amazing picture quality, and you can turn it on using your voice. It's very reliable."

What's the difference?

It's in how she's telegraphing her belief in the TV and using that to persuade you. The first example is passive, both in body language and spoken language. It's someone trying to persuade you to buy something she doesn't know or believe in. The second example is the opposite. The language and physical presence are all about confidence.

Avoid starting your persuasive argument with "I think" or "I feel" and make a declarative statement instead. Because frankly, no one cares what you think or feel in that moment. With persuasion, it's not about your feelings; it's about theirs.

It matters who your audience is, though.

"I guarantee this TV will work" only works if you have a reputation that can back up the guarantee. "This TV is guaranteed to work" is language that works when people don't know your reputation, but they are willing to follow your confidence and strong belief.

Confidence isn't easy to come by.

Think of dating. Sure, great looks might be the hook, but confidence carries the show. A great-looking guy afraid of his own shadow isn't great-looking for long. The most attractive quality of a person is their confidence. It overrides everything else over time.

And that means that confidence sells.

People want to be around confident people because we're attracted to confidence. We'll follow someone who's confident. You could have ten people completely lost in a building, and it would just take one confident person to say "Let's go this way" to get the whole group to follow. Confidence is crucial to getting people to follow, buy in, and be persuaded.

DON'T BE PERSUADED, USING A LAWYER'S MINDSET

Knowing how a lawyer uses persuasion can be useful in protecting yourself from being manipulated. When it comes to using persuasion to take advantage of people, advertisers and the media are at the top of the list.

Take what I've just laid out and reverse engineer it. That means watching out for emotional hooks, paying attention to language, and understanding when physical presence and confidence are being used to persuade.

Let's start with the emotional tricks that are used to persuade people.

Questions are one of the best ways to get people to think what you want them to think. When you ask the right questions the right way, people come to your conclusion but think they got there on their own. It's one of the reasons I'm careful to never ask something I don't know the answer to. The wrong answer can blow my persuasive case out of the water.

That means you need to listen to the questions someone is using to persuade you. They're probably leading you on a one-way path to a conclusion, so ask them questions that flip the script.

For example, imagine someone is trying to sell you a home security system.

"Do you want your family to be safe? Do you want them protected? Then you need this home alarm system."

"I'm not sure . . ."

"Do you love your family?"

"Yes . . ."

"Here's a list of all your neighbors who have signed up. They care about their family and the neighborhood. Don't you think you should, too?"

"Well I don't . . . I mean, yes, I guess so."

They've told you nothing about the product, its limitations, or the cost. They haven't told you they're just selling you an overpriced keypad. Instead of product specs, they've asked controlled questions and hitched the product to fear and guilt.

"If you don't buy our security system, it's your fault if your family is the victim of a crime," they're basically saying.

It's a false equation built with leading questions. Your emotional response has been completely hijacked, and they've shut off your critical thinking. They're one-path, one-conclusion questions. You break that by asking questions that are off the path.

"Do you want your family to be safe? Do you want them protected?"

"Absolutely. What features does your product offer that can specifically improve what we have now?"

"Um . . ."

Always be wary of someone who is trying to sell you something based on an emotional response. If they're not giving you the facts and just trying to stoke your emotions, walk away. Or if the facts you're given can't be verified, trigger a red flag, because people can mislead with bad data just as easily as emotional manipulation. Whoever controls emotions controls the situation. They control the conclusions people draw and the actions people take. Because yes, if you have a crappy product to sell, just wrap it in fear, jealousy, guilt, or fear of missing out, and you can sell it.

> DON'T AUTOMATICALLY FOLLOW CONFIDENCE; FOLLOW FACTS AND REALITY.

Beyond the emotional manipulation is the pressure to follow someone who seems to have confidence. At the most basic level, just know that you're going to be drawn to confident people and what they say—but don't let their confidence blind you. Don't automatically follow confidence; follow facts and reality.

Overconfidence is a different animal than real confidence. Overconfidence is easier to resist because it's what jerks are made of. Overconfident people are open to attack. Not only are they overestimating their smarts, but people enjoy seeing them get taken down a notch.

Sometimes, I would get a witness who thinks they're going to lie and get away with it because they're the smartest guy in the room. They're smug. They have all the answers ready. And because of that, they're easy to take down.

I start with softball questions, one easy question after another. Overconfident people read their success with those kinds of questions as affirmation of how smart they are.

"Were you at the scene?"

"Yes."

"Did you see the car?"

"Yes."

"Where was it parked?"

"On the street in front of the house."

Then you toss in a tough question. "According to city records, the street was being repaved that day, and any cars would have been towed. So, where was the car parked?"

"Wait, I meant that it was in the driveway . . ."

Overconfidence is a hungry monster. You feed it until it explodes.

ARGUMENT IS NOT PERSUASION

Pride and ego are not the source of real confidence, nor are they a part of ethical persuasion.

Early in life, I struggled with always having to be right, and it was something I had to get past once I became a lawyer. The more overconfident you are, the less people listen to you over time. If you always have to be right, you end up persuading people using unethical methods. When the win becomes more important than anything else, the end justifies the means—even if those means are questionable.

Being right is for your own benefit and not the other person's. If your end goal is to be right and win the argument, the way you get there takes a back seat to that goal. Any method is fair game.

Some lawyers will leverage people's feelings unethically, getting them to make an illogical jump in a way that feels like it makes sense. We see this approach all the time today because it works.

Don't be that guy.

The art of persuasion is powerful, and it shouldn't be used as a weapon to manipulate people's emotions. As a rule of thumb, simply ask yourself any time someone is trying to persuade you, "Who stands to benefit here?" Be leery of situations where all the upside belongs to the other party.

ARGUMENT IS NOT PERSUASION. I CAN GET A PERSON TO SAY I WON, BUT THEY WON'T BE PERSUADED TO CHANGE THEIR MIND OR FOLLOW THROUGH WITH AN ACTION.

You can successfully persuade someone the right way as long as you get rid of the desire to be right all the time. Persuasion doesn't create dupes. Unethical persuasion does.

As a lawyer, my goal is to convince people to see something new for the purpose of helping someone. I'm essentially asking the jury to join me in making the right decision for justice. I'm asking them to become true believers, who follow through with their decision and action.

If I lose sight of that goal and start debating to win and prove I'm right, I'm no longer persuading. I'm arguing. Argument is not persuasion. I can get a person to say I won, but they won't be persuaded to change their mind or follow through with an action.

Persuasion doesn't create enemies. Arguing to prove who's right does.

From the moment you begin the path of persuasion, you have to let go of the argument mindset, the win-even-if-I-have-to-lie approach. Believe in what you're saying, be confident it's solid and true, and lead people down the path to where they can believe it too.

It's only when you've completely sold your case and are standing in front of a new, true believer that you're ready to start negotiating for what you want.

CLOSING REMARKS

Persuasion isn't arguing against people but working with them.

Great persuasion means understanding what people want and like, and how to get them to your conclusion with those things intact. It means understanding that your physical presence and language has an impact on how successful you are.

Persuasion is an art that accepts emotion as a key element, understanding that facts must travel with emotion, often through the power of story, to have any real impact.

When you understand what persuasion is, you can spot when it's being used on (or against) you. You can avoid logical fallacies and false equations trapping you, dissecting them with the same questions you'd use to build a persuasive case in other situations.

Persuasion is understanding that you can change minds when you target hearts first.

CHAPTER 7:
NEGOTIATING

The smallest spark of static electricity can change your entire life.

A young couple, hoping to get some time away and spend the weekend relaxing, had booked a hotel room. They spent the day visiting family and friends, enjoying a nice lunch together, and doing a little shopping before heading back to the hotel.

The woman was tired. She wanted to take a short nap before they made dinner plans.

While she lay asleep on the bed in the room, the man went to the closet by the door and pulled out a box full of small canisters of butane. He gathered a few other things he'd brought with him and went into the bathroom to start making butane honey oil.

Butane honey oil is a concentrated and extremely potent form of marijuana. It sells for more than twenty-five times what regular marijuana sells for, and if you believe what you see on the internet, it's easy to make. Unlike meth, which requires a pile of chemicals and ingredients, it only takes a few to manufacture butane honey oil. The price point and supposed ease of manufacture has led to an epidemic of arrests in California. Marijuana might be legal, but the manufacture of butane honey oil is not.

Yet meth and butane honey oil have one similarity, and that's the danger involved in making it.

Things can go boom quickly.

In the hotel bathroom, things seemed to be going along fine. The man had made butane honey oil once before without any problems, and he'd watched several videos online that explained the easy process. Several canisters of butane later, something happened.

Did the air conditioner in the other room kick in? Did someone walk by in the hallway and stir up static electricity on the carpet outside the couple's door? It's not clear, but the end result was dramatic.

Butane is a great solvent, but it's also a great explosive. It boils at room temperature, and it's ideal for making the concentrated THC product because it's a clear, odorless liquid. Problem is, while it's being used to make the product, it off-gases and sinks to the bottom of the room because it's heavier than air. That means the people making the stuff end up standing in a room full of explosive gas, and they don't even realize it. When butane ignites, it expands rapidly, and a wall of flame and pressure blows out windows and does real damage to anything around.

The seemingly innocuous tube of marijuana and butane gas the man was holding in his hand rapidly expanded, exploding into a wall of fire with flames racing from the bathroom into the main hotel room. His shirtless upper body was badly burned, but he managed to crawl out of a small window in the bathroom.

His girlfriend wasn't as fortunate.

She was trapped in the room for half a minute before being able to get out. Hotel video footage shows her in shock, staggering out to the pool area. She ended up with burns on 90 percent of her body, wheelchair-bound for the rest of her life with significant permanent injury. It was a miracle that either of them survived. They went from having a fun day of relaxation to fighting for their lives in excruciating pain, all in the span of a few hours. What could possibly be worth that much agony?

The internet doesn't tell you this reality. People were convinced it was worth making at home to save on the prices you'd pay at a dispensary. Given the relatively few items needed to make butane honey oil, I saw cases where people were manufacturing it in an apartment, a backyard shed, and even on a park bench.

The cases kept rolling in, and it seemed like the people manufacturing butane honey oil were mostly young people in their late teens or early twenties. Time and again, the nightly news story showed young people blowing things up, including themselves. Permanent disability, painful full-body and internal burns, brain damage. All just to get some cheap, concentrated marijuana.

Even more than the legal concern to prosecute these cases was the pressure to get the message out to people that the manufacture of butane honey oil wasn't worth it. We wanted to stop people from hurting themselves more than anything. There were fifty-five open cases in the county the day the hotel case landed on my desk.

The hotel case bothered me and saddened me at the same time. It was one of the most devastating butane honey oil cases I'd seen yet. The sheer tragedy of it almost took my breath away.

These two people were not violent drug dealers. They weren't hardened criminals; they were young, misguided people with their lives ahead of them. He was still with his girlfriend, functioning as her caretaker. She didn't want him to go to prison, because she needed him to take care of her.

> THAT'S WHEN I REALIZED WE COULD DO MORE THAN JUST PUNISH A PERSON.

The defense approached me wanting to work out a deal, proposing some kind of community service. That's when I realized we could do more than just punish a person. We could actually get real benefit out of this case because it had the *power to persuade* built into it.

You can lock a person away, but true justice is better served if you can use a tragedy to make a positive impact and maybe save a few lives. What if the public knew about this case? What if they had a chance to see real people's lives and how this affected them?

I went to my supervisors to see if we could work out a deal where he'd get some jail time, yes, but with a bigger focus on probation with suspended prison time. In exchange, we'd get an agreement from the defendant and his girlfriend to work with the DA's office and make a movie to get the word out on the dangers of producing butane honey oil. If he messed up, he'd go to prison.

I was pretty sure he wasn't someone who would mess up, but to be sure, when the defense attorney offered to let me sit down with her, her client, and my supervisor, I jumped on it. That's not something a defense attorney is normally going to allow a prosecutor to do, but I'd built up credibility with her in previous cases and she trusted me to do the right thing. Because of the severity of the case, both my supervisors and I wanted to be sure the defendant was a good candidate for what we had in mind.

We both sat down with the defendant and interviewed him. I could see that he was incredibly remorseful about what he'd done to his girlfriend. He expressed genuine regret and took responsibility for what he'd done. On top of all those emotions, he knew he was facing many years in prison. This clearly terrified him because he had never been to prison before.

Justice wasn't putting him in prison and further victimizing the girlfriend by removing her caregiver. Instead, it was making the video to warn others. It took a year to make, but the end result was a powerful video that won awards as the best public service video in California for that year. It also opened doors for speaking opportunities, giving us a chance to present information to communities and spread the word on the danger of butane honey oil. The video took tragedy and directed it toward something positive.

Part of negotiating is realizing what you have and what you don't have.

This was a unique case that suited itself perfectly to a creative solution, but I had to know what I possessed. Tragic story. Sympathetic defendant and victim. No further danger to society. It checked all the boxes.

Yet, if I only saw the case as an opportunity to punish and didn't realize what I possessed, I'd have not only missed out on a bigger return, but I would have extended the tragedy for those two people.

More often than not, I've found that putting creativity into the negotiation is how you get to true justice. When it comes to negotiation, everyone can win.

People often miss that, which is why negotiations become stagnant or combative. It's easy for the DA's office to be all about prison and punishment, but it's my mindset that true justice looks different in each situation. The best solution isn't always sticking someone behind bars. If I can find

WHEN IT COMES TO NEGOTIATION, EVERYONE CAN WIN.

a way to prevent a person from committing crimes in the future, that's what I want.

For example, as a defense attorney, if I have a young client, I'd rather see them get a misdemeanor than a felony because sending them to prison sets them up for failure in the future. No one comes out of prison unchanged, and getting a job as a convicted felon is tough.

Before I get into a negotiation, I ask myself what outcome I want. What am I OK with taking? What am I willing to give up? What is nonnegotiable?

As a prosecutor, I decided what I wanted, and that was my goal. As a defense attorney, my client is part of the equation. I have to talk to them about what they need or expect and let them know what's even viable. My objectives have to align with what they want.

It's in those questions that you start to see the difference between persuading and negotiating. Negotiation has a goal, and you need to clearly define how you're willing to get there.

YOUR LINE IN THE SAND

Negotiation is like a Venn. It's in the area where the circles overlap that you and your opponent can negotiate and both come out with a win.

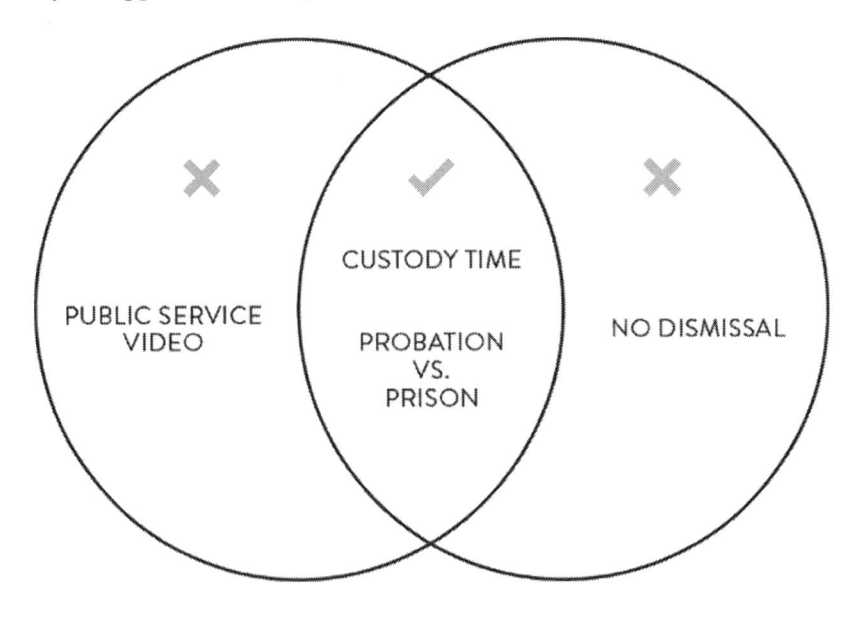

✗ PUBLIC SERVICE VIDEO

✓ CUSTODY TIME
PROBATION VS. PRISON

✗ NO DISMISSAL

Outside of the overlap is another story. The overlap ends at the place you've drawn your proverbial line in the sand. That's where your nonnegotiables start. What's behind the line you will not give up, no matter what.

For the butane honey oil case, it was nonnegotiable for the defendant to get a dismissal. I was insistent that he had to accept responsibility for what had happened. It was also nonnegotiable that he would participate in making the public service video. What was negotiable was the custody time and whether he went to prison or went on probation.

When it comes to negotiation, the other side is drawing their own lines. They know what they will and won't give up. They know what end goal they are looking for.

If both parties have done their homework, the negotiation has a chance to end with two satisfied parties who feel like they've won because they got to their goal, assuming that both sides can at least find some common ground. But if either has failed to define what they're willing to concede and what they absolutely cannot give up, someone is going to come out a loser. If neither side is willing to move, then the negotiations will go nowhere.

Negotiating is an action. Meaning, if one side is unwilling to take action, you're just making demands. Negotiations happen when both sides have things to give up and things to gain. The key is to know where the other side has drawn their line and attempt to get them to move it in the direction you want.

Before every case, I sit down and decide what the most important thing in it is. Is it the conviction? The time in prison? Help and treatment for the person? A change in the plea? This is how I arrive at what I'm willing to give up and what is nonnegotiable. I actually have to sit down and make a decision on these things.

Each case is unique, and it's based on all the work I've done up to that point. The evaluating, critical thinking, and understanding—I'm in no position to start negotiating if I haven't done all of that first, because successful negotiation is only possible if I know what I have and what I want.

TAKE THE DEAL OR GROW OLD IN PRISON

A young family had just moved to town and into a small house on a seemingly quiet street. She was still looking for work, but he'd found a job as an auto mechanic nearby. The money was good, but the new friends her husband had met on the job weren't. They were a consistently bad influence, and it wasn't long before significant problems made their way home with him.

Though he hadn't been a heavy drinker before, his new friends changed that for him. Getting drunk with his co-workers became part of his job, it seemed. While the wife didn't like many of the guys he worked with when they were sober, she despised them when they were drunk. They made her uneasy, and when they'd show up at the house, she never felt safe around them, even if her husband was there. As she described later, they "made my skin crawl, like they were waiting for my husband to be gone so they could do something."

One night, while her husband was out on a beer run and she was sitting in the dark living room watching TV, she was startled by banging and screaming at the front door.

"Let me in! I know you're in there!" came a loud and slightly slurred voice.

She was scared. She recognized the voice as belonging to one of her husband's co-workers, already a few drinks in. Her husband had invited him over but hadn't gotten back yet with the beer.

Keeping the lights off, she quietly made her way to the other end of the house, where the kids' bedrooms were, and sat down on the floor. She could still hear the pounding at the front door and wanted to be with her kids in case anything happened.

There was a loud crack, and the door flew open. They guy had kicked the door in.

Her youngest son woke up. "Mommy, what is it?"

She tried to shush him, but she could hear the man coming down the hallway. Her son started to cry, and her daughter woke up.

"Shh!" she said, crawling onto one of the beds and pulling her kids close. The door to the bedroom jerked open, and she could see the silhouette of the man standing against the light from the hallway night-light.

He had a gun in his hand.

When the husband returned home about twenty minutes later, two cases of beer in hand, he found his front door in splinters and a drunken co-worker holding his wife and children at gunpoint.

The 911 call brought the police pretty fast. Having a mother and her children held at gunpoint tends to do that. By the time the police had arrived, however, the situation had changed a bit. The husband had managed to convince his co-worker to come out of the house and not hurt his family.

He'd complied, sort of. The kids were left in the bedroom, but he had dragged the wife out by her hair. The flashing police lights created an eerie horror movie scene where a huge man with a weapon was holding a woman against her will. When this arrived on my desk back when I was a prosecutor, it was a serious case that I was intent on prosecuting.

Kidnapping? False imprisonment? Assault with a gun? Yes on all of them, for each victim. And whenever you get a gun involved, there's a ton of enhancements that get added to the pile. The defendant was looking at a long stretch in prison.

The husband was hemming and hawing a bit. He didn't want to lose his job or get in trouble with his other co-worker buddies, so he was trying to downplay what happened. But the wife was having none of it. She stuck to her story. She'd been terrorized, and she was still feeling it.

Negotiation on this case took a different angle than it did with the butane honey oil case. Different scenario, different facts, and a much different defendant. At best, I was willing to go with fifteen to twenty years as the minimum.

The defense could take the deal or go to trial and get something much worse; that was my offer. I wasn't going to concede much at all, because what he'd done had caused real trauma to people. The defense should've negotiated and taken the offer, but of course, the defendant took the latter approach.

I'd laid out my nonnegotiables, and they'd rejected all of them.

Essentially, they refused to come to the negotiating table. There was no overlap in what we wanted, and the defendant decided that taking a gamble in the courtroom to get something better than what I was offering was the best route rather than adjusting his line in the sand so negotiation could happen. The man eventually went to trial and was convicted, and I'm sure he was wishing he had taken a twenty-year deal when it had been offered to him. Now, he won't be out of prison until he's a senior citizen.

When you come to the table without much to offer, you'd better be able to recognize the reality of the worst-case scenario and adjust your line in the sand.

WHAT DOES YOUR OPPONENT WANT?

Negotiating isn't mind reading, but it's close.

As a defense attorney, I have to know what my client wants out of a case. I'm negotiating for them, but it's their case. I can't assume I know what they want, so I have to ask them those same questions about what they want. I need to know what their goals are and what they will and won't give up. What I want to see happen at the end of the day doesn't matter if it doesn't line up with what they want.

In a negotiation, you need to know what all the players want.

A client isn't an opponent, but they are a player. At least I can talk to them and know for sure what they want. For a true opponent, I can't simply go and ask them what they want. Their goals and nonnegotiables are going to be held close to their chest. That secrecy is its own bargaining chip during the negotiation.

> IN A NEGOTIATION, YOU NEED TO KNOW WHAT ALL THE PLAYERS WANT.

Since I'm not a mind reader, I have to figure out what an opponent wants on my own. What are the facts of the situation? How are they operating? Are they relying on emotion and all worked up, or are they level-headed and logical? What do I know about their reputation when it comes to negotiation? What will they likely compromise on?

And once again, we can learn from the game of poker. In particular, the concept of looking for someone who's bluffing by noticing their tells.

I know, for example, that when a prosecutor is pulling jail calls, they're probably doing it because they feel their case is weak. They need some extra evidence to boost their case or are hoping to catch a break somewhere in those call recordings. If they're struggling to put together a solid case, that lets me know I have some room for negotiation.

Sometimes you spot bluffs simply by having done your own research.

GREED BLINDS YOU TO SEEING A GOOD DEAL WHEN IT'S OFFERED.

"Here's the deal I'm willing to offer," I might say to an opposing lawyer. "Not good enough. We're not afraid to go to trial."

Well, sir, I happen to know that in twenty years of practicing law, you've never been to trial, and I've done over forty trials, so let's go to trial. Because I'm almost certain that you're bluffing.

This is about understanding the person. If you're not good at reading people, you can at least do research and get the best understanding possible. You can see what deals they've made in the past and what people have said about them.

In particular, be on the lookout for a greedy negotiator.

Obviously, you don't want to be one yourself. The line in the sand isn't just to keep your opponent from crossing; it's also to keep you from overreaching. It's easy to get caught up into a double or nothing mindset when you think you've got the upper hand. They agreed to your terms, your nonnegotiables are safe, and you met your goal . . . but you still want more.

That's a great way to get burned.

Greed blinds you to seeing a good deal when it's offered. You have to know when to stop, take the deal, or get out. Timing is critical in negotiation because a great deal won't be on the table forever. Your opponent can change their mind, or the circumstances can change.

If you have everything you want, seal the deal right then. Finalize it before they talk to someone who will change their mind. Get their signature on the line before they come across someone who will give them a better deal because if there's no signature, there's no deal. Your negotiation isn't finished. Got a good deal that meets your parameters? Take it. Don't panic. Just take the deal. There is no reason to second-guess if you already know what you want.

DON'T WING IT; FIND SOLID GROUND

The only thing that can blow a great deal out of the water faster than greed is a lack of preparation. You walk into a negotiation without preparation, and your opponent is figuring that out every minute that ticks by on the clock. Your lack of preparation gives them more bargaining chips.

"This is the deal I will offer."

"You can't prove *this thing*, so there's no way I'd take that deal."

Guess what? If I'm not prepared and don't know if I can or can't prove *this thing*, they would be right. They shouldn't take the deal. I'm bluffing from a weak position. But if I know I can prove *this thing*?

My deal is solid and I won't be moved.

Wherever you aren't prepared, you have to bluff. You have to take a leap into the dark and hope you land on something solid.

There was a drug case that illustrates this perfectly.

I was in the midst of a heavy caseload at the DA's office when a meth case landed on my desk. A guy got picked up with the drugs, and he had a couple of cell phones with him. I was pretty busy at the time, but even a cursory amount of preparation before meeting the defense attorney told me that a) the meth was obviously illegal, and b) having multiple cell phones was strange and indicated something was up.

The confiscated drugs didn't come to a huge amount. Since I hadn't had a chance to review the call records of the defendant, I decided to negotiate on what I knew for sure and just stick to a simple felony possession and not press further for sales or any other charges. By skipping charges for sales, I was giving the defendant a great deal and likely sparing him from the more serious consequences that came with being charged with intent to sell. At that time, any prior sales convictions could be brought into consideration if another sales charge was added, greatly expanding potential prison sentences.

I thought my offer was fair, but the defense attorney thought otherwise. She didn't like the offer at all.

"In the county where I practice, we don't do that," she said, apparently forgetting the county her client was arrested in was a different jurisdiction. "I don't think this is worth a felony. I want a misdemeanor."

That was the first problem I picked up on right away. She was negotiating for what *she* wanted instead of going to her client and asking him what he wanted.

"This offense deserves a felony sentence," I told her, and let her know that I wouldn't relinquish this point. "You should take the deal."

She refused, continuing to press for a misdemeanor.

"This is all I'm willing to offer," I told her again.

I was negotiating purely on what I knew, no bluffing, which meant I wasn't including those call records that I had yet to check. They had the potential to prove far more damning things. Plus, I took into account the time and resources it would take to prepare this case for trial. An early but fair resolution based on the facts I had would be a win for all involved. The defense attorney should have picked up on all of that and seen that the deal I had offered was actually a good one for the defendant.

"If you do not take this deal, I will pull it off the table," I told the defense attorney. "I will also pull this person's phone records and check their calls and text messages. I'm going to find out if he was selling."

She did not relent.

I went on. "You should talk to your client and tell him what I'm going to do, that I'm going to find out if he was selling meth. You should take the simple felony possession now."

The defense attorney rejected the deal.

Fine by me. I got a search warrant and I pulled those phone records. And I hit the jackpot, just as I suspected I would. On the next court date, I informed the judge of a change to the complaint. "Your honor, I'm going to be amending the complaint at this point so that it now reads drug sales, and I'm adding these drug sales priors because he has prior convictions."

Negotiations were over. We were going to trial, and to show drug sales were taking place, I now had reviewed the cell phone texting records and had an expert ready to testify.

The text messages alone were pretty strong.

"You got any crystal?"

"You know I do. How much you want this time?"

"The usual."

"Meet me at the parking lot in 30. Don't forget my money."

The defense attorney overstepped her line, if she ever had one. She went double or nothing, and that greed cost her client a long prison term. When I offered her the deal, she either didn't understand how weak her position was or decided to gamble.

Preparing for negotiation is like a two-pronged attack. The first is that you have to research, gather information, and understand what you have to deal with. The second is knowing where you stand.

For the initial negotiation, I knew where I stood.

Yeah, I was fairly sure the defendant was selling meth based on the location he was found, the quantity of drugs he had with him, the phones, and just the whole nature of it. But I didn't negotiate based on that hunch, because during the initial negotiation, I hadn't had time to gather that evidence yet. I didn't draw my line in the sand based on a guess. I only used what I was sure of. It gave me solid ground to make a deal on, and I didn't have any sense of panic over a bluff gone bad.

If you don't understand the two parts to preparing for a negotiation, you have to rely on bluffing.

You might get a good hand and pull it off. Or you might fail spectacularly. You can only guess whether it's a good deal, and it's a struggle to know whether to take the deal or walk away. Bluffing is for gambling. Negotiation calls for facts and solid ground.

> BLUFFING IS FOR GAMBLING. NEGOTIATION CALLS FOR FACTS AND SOLID GROUND.

KNOW WHEN THE GROUND SHIFTS

Solid ground might make you feel confident until there's an earthquake that shakes both the ground and your confidence. In California, we know all about earthquakes, and we also know about constantly changing laws.

Every January the changes to California law go into effect, and as a lawyer, you'd better be paying attention. In 2021, one of the changes involved probation on misdemeanor cases. Previously, you could go three years on probation for a misdemeanor, but after January, that was reduced to only one year on most misdemeanor cases.

You can bet that new piece of information affected how and when I would negotiate.

A few months before the change went into place, I began preparation for a case that was going to trial. But I knew what would happen in January, and so I requested a January trial date. Based on the work I'd done on the case, I was pretty sure there would be a plea agreement, and so I decided to hold off negotiating anything for my client until the changes went into effect. Instead of being offered three years probation, he had to be offered one.

Shifting ground doesn't have to mean you're thrown off-balance. It simply means you reassess and calculate it into your negotiation preparation. You might adjust your goal. Your negotiables might change. You might move your line because your position has become weaker or stronger.

Nearly every situation is dynamic in some way. Something is always going to change slightly, and if you understand this reality and figure out how to use it, you end up with a better context for influencing the outcome.

In most negotiations, there's an exchange. Each party gives and each party gets. Understanding the shifting legal ground gave me more flexibility when it came to making a deal. I didn't waste a bargaining chip on reducing the years of probation; it was coming on its own anyway.

Negotiation where each party walks away feeling that they got a win never happens on the fly. It starts by getting facts together and understanding the situation and your opponent. You use this to define your goal, an acceptable outcome that you can live with, by determining what you will and will not give up.

Next, you have to understand what it is you possess because those possessions are your bargaining chips. They're the currency used in a negotiation, what you exchange for what you want.

If you have all that in place, you're on solid ground.

You don't have to bluff.

You don't have to worry if the ground moves a bit.

You will know a good deal when you see it.

In a negotiation done well, both parties can get some kind of win.

But sometimes negotiations fall apart. The reason I've done forty trials as a prosecutor was that forty defense attorneys didn't take the deal I offered. And I'm thankful to say that I didn't win all forty trials.

Sure, making a deal feels good because we all like to win. But it's in my losses that I've banked the experiences I need to be an ever better negotiator because as you'll see, when you lose, you learn.

And that's its own kind of win.

CLOSING REMARKS

Negotiating starts when you know the line you will not cross. On one side are the things you're willing to concede, and on the other, the things you will not.

To draw that line, you might think of negotiation like a poker game. Know what your definition of a win is, and then look at the cards you're holding. What do you have, and what's missing? Know how many bargaining chips you have because your negotiation is limited by what you can bargain with. Pay attention to your opponent to determine if they're bluffing. And then, know when the ground shifts. New information can change your and your opponent's hands. Both of you are playing the same game.

A greedy negotiator loses more than they win, so don't overplay your hand. Don't move that line on a bluff. If neither side is willing to concede anything, there is no negotiation.

Once you get what you want, seal the deal before it's gone.

CHAPTER 8:
WINNING AND LOSING

The ace of spades sailed through the air and landed on the pile of poker chips. The crowd standing around the table gasped, and then erupted into cheers. That was the final card, the one that finished a royal flush, the one that beat a straight flush and four eights. It was the impossible hand.

This was all in a movie, of course, where those kinds of things happen. The 1994 film *Maverick* was a story of con artists and bad luck—but it ended with the best of all luck for the title character, Bret Maverick.

If you're a Texas Hold'em poker player, you don't hold out much hope for a Maverick moment. You'd have to play a game a day for about eighty years to get an unbeatable royal flush. But there are other ways to win at the table. Four aces is a solid hand, with odds of one in every 4,165 hands. Only a straight flush (one in about 72,000 hands) or a royal flush would top it. Those four aces, with their more favorable odds, are such a good hand that the chances of losing a game of poker while holding those cards are pretty slim.

It does happen, though, and not just in the movies.

During the 2008 World Series of Poker, players Justin Phillips and Motoyuki Mabuchi were facing off at the table, with Mabuchi going all in as he yelled "gamble!", pushing his chips to the center of the table. He had four aces and he, like anyone else, was sure it was a win.

Except for Justin Phillips who, like Maverick, had a royal flush.

The ESPN announcers excitedly pointed out that it was a statistical improbability—about one in 2.7 billion—that these two hands would show up at the same table. And there's the truth: you can have four aces and feel like winning is a sure thing, only to see it literally flushed away.

I've learned that many times as a lawyer, both in experience and in observation. No matter what amount of evidence or proof there is, no matter how many people swear the case is a sure thing, the truth is that any trial can be lost.

There's always some other component going on besides evidence and legal definitions. Juries are made up of twelve people I've never met before, with twelve different life histories, twelve different emotional responses, twelve different opinions and worldviews. These are all massive variables.

You can't be certain when the human factor is involved. The jury can be told that they have a duty and obligation to follow the law, but jury nullification is real. That's where a jury decides to make a statement about something and flat out chooses not to follow the law. The jury's verdict sends a message. Remember the road rage case where the man was followed for four miles and beaten up, where I even had video to show what happened? The jury chose not to convict because they didn't like the victim, who was a sex offender.

At the end of the day, jurors aren't lawyers. They're everyday people. If something doesn't feel right, they'll vote against it as a crime. It's the whole issue of the interplay between emotional thinking and critical thinking; you can't be all in on one or the other.

It's easy as a prosecutor to forget all of that is a factor and instead get caught up in evidence. "Well, the law says this, I have the evidence to prove it, so it's a solid win."

And then you meet the jury.

WHEN EVERYTHING IS ABOUT WINNING, YOU'RE NOT OPEN TO LEARNING.

The supposed slam dunk, in-home crotch grab case was only my third case as a prosecutor, and I can honestly say I'm glad I got a loss like that early in my career.

There's a strange thing that happens when you have a winning streak. If you're not careful, you can become someone who cares more about preserving the winning streak at any cost rather than doing the best ethical job you can, even if it means you might not win. When everything is about winning, you're not open to learning.

And when you're dealing with juries, you have to learn.

WHEN A CRIME DOESN'T FEEL LIKE ONE

Some of the most difficult cases to prosecute are marijuana DUI cases.

I've had cases as a prosecutor where someone clearly under the influence of marijuana brought back a hung jury. The evidence was clear. Each jury member could check off a box for every legal definition being met. I'd proven the defendant was operating a motor vehicle under the influence of the drug.

What's the problem?

Some people don't see driving under the influence of marijuana as an issue.

Most publicity and press about the dangers of driving under the influence has been about alcohol, not marijuana. You don't hear that driving under the influence of marijuana is just as dangerous as driving while drunk. You don't hear of high drivers killing people on the road; you only hear about drunk drivers.

We have a laid-back image of people high on marijuana. We have years of movies that portray marijuana users as innocuous, even worth a few Cheech-and-Chong laughs. The worst they do is get the munchies. What's the harm, right?

"Alcohol has a legal limit. What's the legal limit on marijuana?"

"There's no legal limit."

"Why are we even here talking about this?"

In a way, the law itself reflects this dilemma. Regarding driving under the influence, alcohol has two separate laws in California. You can prosecute someone for driving under the influence even if under the legal limit of consumption, as well as over. Marijuana, on the other hand, is different. Everyone is impacted differently. Were they really under the influence? Did it really impact their driving? It's hard to prove.

Another example of something a jury might not view as a crime is child abuse. We all hate child abuse, so that kind of case should be open-and-shut, right? Except something called *unreasonable discipline* is included in that. Defining unreasonable discipline is fairly subjective.

"You touch your child at all, you're going down!" might be one juror's opinion.

"Growing up, I got the belt all the time. What's the big deal?" might be another juror's opinion.

People come from different walks of life. The law might put down some parameters, but people aren't going to see it the same. You can try to flesh that out as you choose your jury, but people sneak through all the time because there's no way you can completely understand a person in a ten-minute examination. Plus, people sometimes have an agenda, and not everything they tell you is honest.

You can have a solid case in every which way, but then the human element knocks your feet out from under you and you lose. It happens.

THE CASE OF THE CONFUSED SPEAKER

There are still moments where I relish the win, don't get me wrong. Sometimes that unpredictable human element can swing toward the win column.

Take, for example, the case of the confused speaker.

A worker at a car dealership spotted a sound system in a car that he liked. It had high-end speakers, the kind you install in the trunk. The car was in the dealership's repair shop getting a fuel pump replaced, so removing the speaker system from the trunk was easy.

The worker removed the speaker and put it in his own car, but his boss noticed the customer's car was missing the speaker it had arrived with. Surveillance footage showed that the worker had walked to the trunk of the car, but it didn't have an angle on what he was doing. The worker realized that his employer was onto him, but since he still wanted the nice speaker, he hastily replaced the stolen speaker in the customer's car with the low-end speaker from his own car. Shortly after the worker had completed the swap, his employers confronted him about a missing speaker. They opened up his trunk and removed the stolen speaker. But then, they were confused when they returned to the customer's car and found another speaker already there in the trunk.

Rather than try to get to the bottom of what happened, they just took the stolen speaker from the worker's car, kept the worker's original speaker too, and then fired him on the spot. At trial, this confusion over the two speakers destroyed the employer's credibility, making it look like they might have just been setting up the worker or firing him for no good reason.

It wasn't looking good as far as winning this case was concerned, but then the defendant himself threw me a bone and decided to testify to solidify his case. I knew that was my moment, and I cross-examined him in every direction. Talk about your confused speakers.

"So you said you were working on the car," I stated.

"Yes," he said.

"What were you working on?"

"I was working on replacing the fuel pump."

"Surveillance footage shows you in the trunk of the car. Is the fuel pump in the trunk of the car?"

"No . . ."

Instead of just leaving things as they were, with the right amount of confusion to provide reasonable doubt to the jury, he got up on the stand and was forced to provide an answer as to why he was in the trunk of the car. It didn't take long to give the jury a sense that the defendant was making some stuff up. What he was saying made no sense in light of what the jury had already learned. They came back with a guilty verdict.

Afterward, when the defense attorney got a chance to speak with the jury, they told him that they were all planning on a not guilty verdict until the defendant opened his mouth.

"We knew within ten minutes your guy was lying," they said.

That case was a win for me, but it was a difficult one. I was on the path to losing because the testimony of the employer, and his confusion over the different speaker, damaged my case. When I finished presenting my case, I knew I'd failed to convince the jury. I could see it in their body language.

In a trial, each lawyer direct examines their own witnesses and has the opportunity to cross-examine the opposing side's witnesses. There are times where I might not want to cross-examine a particular witness, such as when my questioning of an expert witness might bore the jury, or when I really have nothing to gain. Cross-examination is a tool that is used to expose, uncover, or reveal information that didn't come out on direct examination. It's the tool lawyers use to ensure that their side of the story gets heard as well.

In the end, for this case, it all came down to how I cross-examined the witness.

INTUITION AND REPUTATION COME WITH EXPERIENCE

It's not unusual to have a moment in a case when you get a gut feeling that everything hinges on one thing.

Something comes out in testimony, or something unexpected happens, and you know that's the death blow. Like when a judge allows the defense to let the jury know the victim is a convicted sex offender. Or a witness gets up and admits he didn't see someone actually driving drunk, but knows the person does it often and wants to get them in trouble.

I had a domestic abuse case as a prosecutor with all the evidence you could ask for—threatening text messages and a voicemail, a recording of a frantic 911 call—and yet, for some reason, the victim went up on the stand and explained it all away as faked text messages and a big joke.

I don't know why the victim did that.

I couldn't control what they said on the stand.

All I could do was present the case the best I could, with clear evidence and an explanation of the scenario. When I lay the case out in an organized and persuasive fashion and the jury comes back with a not guilty, it's not on me. The jury decided to believe a far more fantastical story than the one that fit the evidence. That was their decision.

Sometimes no amount of preparedness or persuasion will change someone's mind, and you have to know when to throw in the towel. The more cases I try and the more experience I get in trial, the more I'm able to identify when this is happening.

You build your intuition through experience. And it's that intuition that goes off during a trial when you sense a turning point you hadn't predicted.

You can try and compensate for what pops up, but sometimes you can't correct it and pull out a win. At best, you might try to resolve the case through a deal. Whatever happens, you can't take it personally, and you can't cross ethical boundaries.

As I've mentioned, my reputation as an attorney is one of the pieces on the board whenever I go to trial. It has to do with credibility and trust, which affects how judges, other attorneys, and the jury view the cases I present. I know that I'll be working with many of these same people in the future. I'm not looking to burn bridges.

In light of that, I always give every case my best effort. I certainly want to win. But at the end of the day, if the jury won't go along with me, that's how it is. I'm not going to push the boundaries of ethics to eke out a win every time. A win that results in a miscarriage of justice isn't a win; it's an injustice.

> YOU BUILD YOUR INTUITION THROUGH EXPERIENCE.

People talk. Word gets around. Judges talk to other judges, lawyers talk to other lawyers. If you become known as someone who will compromise your integrity in a case, it's going to haunt you.

One story I heard of was a domestic violence case in which a woman was horribly beaten by her boyfriend. This wasn't the boyfriend's first time in the ring; he was known to have a nasty temper.

The evidence in the case was sparse, and the DA's office had their work cut out for them because, despite being subpoenaed, the victim never showed up at trial. Over and over, they tried to get a hold of her, but no luck. That left the DA's office relying on 911 calls, witness testimony, and every other related thing they were allowed to introduce into trial.

Amazingly, the defendant was still convicted despite the lack of personal testimony from the victim about what happened. Sentencing was set for a week later and wouldn't you know it, on that day, the victim managed to make her way to court.

"Please don't send my boyfriend to prison!" she begged. She kept repeating herself, asking the court to show mercy in the sentencing.

The judge, not missing the fact that the victim had been AWOL during the entire trial, confronted her. "How is that you can show up for sentencing, but not be here once during the trial?"

"The defense attorney told me it would be better if I didn't show up," she said.

You could see the reactions on everyone's face in the courtroom, from the judge down to the attorneys and courtroom staff.

The defense attorney whirled around and looked at the woman. "Excuse me?! Who told you that?"

"Someone at your office," she said.

"I want a name," he said.

"I can't remember." She began backpedaling her claim.

It's a lot harder for the prosecution if the victim doesn't show up, so I have no doubt that someone in that attorney's office told her that. What we had was an attempt to suppress a material witness in a case. That's going to get talked about. That's going to be remembered.

That's winning at any cost. Why would that be worth it?

You don't know if the cost you're paying will even get you a win with all the uncontrollable variables. That defense attorney ended up losing. He, or someone in his office, put his credibility and reputation on the line for that case.

> WINNING AT ANY COST IS A TERRIBLE LIFE MOTTO.

Winning at any cost is a terrible life motto. Some costs far overshadow the win in the long run.

LEARN FROM OTHERS' LOSSES

It was April 12, 1961, and the United States space program was filled with heads hung low. The Soviet Union had just launched the first human into space. This was during the Cold War, so the news sent shivers down the spines of Americans everywhere. If the Soviets could win the space race, what else could they win?

The US suffered a major loss on the world stage in 1961, but that was when President John F. Kennedy dug in his heels and tasked Vice President

Lyndon Johnson with a big job: create a "space program which promises dramatic results in which we could win." Fast forward to 1962, and JFK is standing in front of over forty thousand at Rice University, making one of the most famous speeches in modern history. He told the people that by the end of the decade, we would put a man on the moon.

JFK continued, feeding off the crowd's energy. "We choose to go to the moon in this decade, not because that will be easy, but because it will be hard . . . because that challenge is one . . . we intend to win." Seven years later, the first humans planted an American flag on lunar soil, making good on that bold declaration.

In the long run, your losses can be the bigger win. JFK and NASA turned a loss in the space race into the rocket fuel our country needed to win an even greater victory. What's more impressive: a guy floating around the planet, or space pioneers landing a rocket ship on the moon taking one small step for man, one giant leap for mankind?

It's impossible to understand the lessons in our losses if we maintain a narrow definition of what a win is. A win gets added to the tally; a loss gets dissected. Losing stings, and you tend to reflect on it much more than you do a win.

I remember every single case I have lost, and I've learned something from each of them. I've learned that nothing is a sure thing, and you're at the mercy of what other people say or do. I've learned I have to double-check things (like evidence being brought into the courtroom). I've learned people are hard to predict.

Whatever the reason for losing, there's one sure thing: it's a fantastic learning experience if you let it teach you. You get a sense of your current boundaries and realize where you still have to grow. Winning all the time makes you complacent; you think you have nothing left to learn. It can also make you overconfident, make you think you can't lose. Or it can even make you stop listening because you're always the smartest person in the room.

It's not just my own losses I can learn from, but others'. Anyone with a competitive nature (like most lawyers) can spot where a win could've been had. As mentioned earlier in this book, part of preparing for a case is considering the angles an opponent might use against my case. There are a few cases I've tried as a prosecutor that I've won, but I could also see a way the defense could have gotten the win.

But just because I can see a path for the defense to win doesn't mean they do.

I was prosecuting a butane honey oil case where a search of the defendant's house had turned up the tools and materials involved in the manufacture. Investigators had also found a couple of drops of honey oil in a plastic container.

Seems like a solid win, right? And for me, it was. We got a conviction in that case, and I'm sure the defendant was good for it. There was other evidence not allowed in trial that clearly indicated manufacture and sales were taking place.

But the defense could have won also.

What was allowed in the trial was weak. As the prosecutor, I had to show that the defendant had manufactured the stuff. Having the equipment and the honey oil on their own didn't necessarily mean they were manufacturing. It's the manufacturing that's the crime.

The tools were in a dusty old box, making it clear they hadn't been used for a while. The few drops of honey oil were pretty sparse and in a beat-up, old plastic container. Neither the drops nor the plastic container looked like something terribly recent.

If I was the defense, I would've questioned the quantity, and how and where it was found.

"Such a tiny little drop," I would've argued. "We don't know it was manufactured from all this equipment. It could've come from anywhere."

From there, I would've made sure the jury understood that the prosecutor had to prove the defendant had actually manufactured the honey oil, and since the equipment was so dusty and the actual drops were fairly crusty, it was very possible he hadn't.

As the prosecutor, I actually saw this as a difficult case. All the defense had to do was take that approach, and they stood a good chance of winning. But they didn't. The defense took a very broad approach and simply pressed the jury to broadly consider whether the evidence was enough. A good defense, but perhaps not the best.

In that case, what I learned was that I had to be able to identify what a case hinged on, and that broad approaches aren't always the best for winning. Who knows? Maybe homing in on the specific "is this enough to prove manufacture?" would have won the case for the defense. It's a fine distinction between the two, but in some cases, you have to help the jury get to the specific point the case hinges on.

There are cases I've lost that I believe I should've won, and there are cases I've won where I see how I could've lost. The key is to always be learning from what did and did not happen that got you to that end result.

MISTAKES THAT SHOULD NOT BE REPEAT OFFENDERS

There are some mistakes I'm only going to make once, like trusting someone to get the right evidence bag without checking it first. Or asking a witness about the value of drugs and then having to fumble around for a calculator while the jury looks on.

Those are mistakes of relinquishing control by putting trust where I shouldn't have and not being prepared. Those mistakes felt awful at the time; they were in my power to avoid, and I never want to put myself in that position again.

Of course, sometimes even if you're prepared and haven't misplaced trust, mistakes still happen.

Early on when I was prosecuting drug cases, I had more experienced attorneys tell me that I always needed to ask my officers if they knew what a usable quantity of drugs was before putting them on the stand.

In order to be considered in possession of drugs, there is a defined amount that must be found. It can't be just a dusting or some residue. It has to be any amount that can be manipulated with your fingers. If you can touch it, roll it, or fill it, it's a usable quantity. It doesn't take very much. It might not be an effective dose, but it's a question of whether it can be used.

The reason I was told to make sure officers knew the definition of a usable quantity was that if they got up on the stand and couldn't provide the answer, that crucial element toward conviction would crumble.

I had a meth case where two officers found a pipe and meth on the defendant. Before the trial, I made sure to talk to the officer who was going to testify.

"Do you know what a usable quantity is?" I asked.

"Yeah, sure," he said.

"Well, what is it?" I asked. I'd just been burned by trusting the officer in the drug evidence case without following up, so I wasn't going to do that again. Trust, but verify.

"It's any amount that can be manipulated," he said.

Great. We were ready for him to testify. His partner sat next to me at the table while I began asking him questions in front of the jury.

"Did you pull over the defendant's car?" I asked.

"Yeah."

"When you searched him, what did you find?"

"The pipe with the meth," he said.

"Are you familiar with what a usable quantity is?"

"Yeah."

"Could you tell the court what a usable quantity is?"

"Any amount that can be used."

No. No, that's not the right answer. I paused and tried again. "What is a usable quantity?"

"Any amount that can be used."

I could tell this was going nowhere, so I ended questioning of that officer and called the more experienced partner up to the stand.

"What is a usable quantity?"

"Any amount that can be manipulated."

Thank you. "Was this a usable quantity?"

"Yes."

"How do you know?"

"I was able to hold it up in my fingers and move it around."

Later, when I asked the first officer what had happened, all he could tell me was that he got nervous.

I was prepared for the trial. I asked the witness beforehand to be sure he knew what he was talking about, and he verified that he did. Yet this still happened. If I hadn't had his partner there to fix the mistake on the stand, the case could've gone south.

The human element is always unpredictable. It's the only sure takeaway when it comes to juries and witnesses. But everything has a teachable moment, so what I learned from this was to talk a witness through potential nervousness. I want to prepare them for the questions I'll be asking for their benefit, not just for my own verification that they know the information.

And then, to just understand that this can still happen.

Because the reality is, as prepared and verified as I can be, there's still the moment where you have to rely on another person to do their job, and sometimes it goes sideways.

> **THE HUMAN ELEMENT IS ALWAYS UNPREDICTABLE.**

I've had cases given to me at the DA's office that someone else prepared and, for whatever reason, were reassigned to me.

"Happy Friday. Here's a new case. You'll be trying it on Monday."

I can't describe the dread I felt as I looked through a "prepared" case, and it wasn't at all what I would have done. Photos were missing. Transcriptions weren't done. Witnesses weren't subpoenaed. In some instances, I'd had to go to the supervisor.

"This isn't a prepared case. It's not remotely ready for trial. It's full of holes."

It stinks going into a case with someone else's preparation knowing you're probably going to lose. One of the reasons I went to a supervisor on record about the problems in the case was so they could brace for a loss. If everyone thinks I was handed off a great and fully prepared case and I went and lost it, that would hurt my reputation.

Calling out shoddy preparation is going to come with some social fallout, but you don't want to wager your reputation in the courtroom on someone else's preparation. Losing someone else's battle is frustrating.

WHAT WINNING LOOKS LIKE

Sometimes winning is not about the destination but about the journey. For example, I was once on a hike at Zion National Park with my wife's family.

We decided to climb Angels Landing, a grueling hike soaring high over the red rocks that rim the valley. The final pitch to the summit is so narrow that hikers have to use a chain to hold on so they don't plummet hundreds of feet to their death (which has happened thirteen times in the last twenty years, by the way).

Our hike ended high up on the trail, where we still had stunning views of the canyon below. But we stopped short of the chains on the final ascent. Why? Because for me it was about the experience, not the destination. We got to see something beautiful that required determination to get as far as we did, and we had the opportunity to bond as we tackled this grueling challenge together. A win can look different depending on how you choose to view it. Experiencing the sheer beauty of Zion National Park was a rich bonding experience with my family I'll never forget.

But today, it's easy to have a cartoon idea of what winning looks like.

We're told winners are like superheroes with magic powers who summit every mountain. This is obviously not reality. Only a correct image of what winning and winners look like will keep you pressing forward.

In 52 BC, Julius Caesar had nearly conquered all of Gallic (French) territory. There was one final decisive battle the Battle of Alesia, where Caesar had to face down a band of holdouts led by Vercingetorix.

The Gauls were a fierce foe, and the Battle of Alesia wasn't going to be easy. Alesia was a small, fortified city at the top of a hill. Caesar didn't have enough men to take the fort, so he formed a circle of trenches and siege works around it. Then, because he realized Vercingetorix was waiting for reinforcements to arrive, he had his troops form another circle outside this to ward off any potential incoming Gallic troops.

Sure enough, the Gauls came to the aid of their fellow tribesmen, and the battle began to look like a loss for Caesar. The Gauls found the weakest spots to attack and gained ground, outnumbering the Romans four to one. It was a weary siege, and the Romans were struggling to hold back the Gauls, much less defeat them.

But then Caesar himself joined in the battle.

One of Rome's top leaders, putting himself in absolute danger, riding out to fight with weary Roman soldiers. He could easily have been killed.

SO MUCH ABOUT WINNING IS HOW YOU LOOK AT A SITUATION, AND HOW YOU LOOK AT YOURSELF AND WHAT YOU'RE WORTH.

When his troops saw him in the thick of the fight, helping them hold the line, they rallied. The victory at Alesia gave Rome the Gallic territory.

It wasn't the impressive Roman siege works that brought about the final moment of victory. It wasn't the walls, the defenses, or the planning. It was a leader who was willing to literally get down into the trenches and fight alongside the soldiers.

You have to be willing to get in the trenches.

Winning rarely looks on from afar, and when it does, it's winning that doesn't gain experience or reputation. You don't learn as much from a distance, and you don't earn respect from a distance.

You have to be willing to do the dirty work and the heavy lifting.

Tolkien's *The Lord of the Rings* trilogy depicts a multilayered win. Not only was the evil enemy defeated, but it was done so by characters who shouldn't have been able to win much of anything. The odds were completely stacked against them.

Physical disparity. Cultural discord. Conflict between tribes and groups. Past history not easily forgotten. A division among the team. An enemy with seemingly unending strength, and minions that completely outnumbered them. And yet the fate of Middle-earth rested in the hands of nine characters, with everyone trusting that one little hobbit would succeed in his task as they kept their focus on completing their own tasks.

There's no unimportant person when it comes to winning. We all have a role to play and an opportunity for victory.

So much about winning is how you look at a situation, and how you look at yourself and what you're worth. Do you think you're too important to get your hands dirty? Do you think you're too unimportant to even have a chance? Do you let a loss beat you down to the point where you don't try to win anymore?

Don't underestimate your value and your ability to win. You don't need to be the smartest or strongest or luckiest. You don't need to have superpowers. You simply need to be the best-prepared and not willing to give up. My grandmother used to say, "where there's a will, there's a way."

When David faced Goliath, he wasn't focused on the nine-foot giant he had against him. He was focused on what he had going for him. He had faith in God and a slingshot.

Yet the whole situation is terrifying if you really think about that moment. So why wasn't David terrified?

Confidence is the best antidote for fear. David had spent years building a relationship with God. He'd protected his sheep from wild animals, like lions and bears. Having that faith and experience gave him the confidence he needed.

On that day, David evaluated the situation with Goliath. He understood the danger and what was at stake, but he also knew what was needed to defeat the giant: faith, preparedness, and a willingness to act. Weak faith would never have allowed David onto that battlefield. Poor preparation would have limited what he could do to defeat the giant. Acting like everyone else in the army would have been a continuing failure.

He prepared for the showdown, not by allowing others to tell him how to prepare (he rejected King Saul's ill-fitting armor), but instead by using his own approach. He thought critically and was able to persuade them to let him face down the literal giant problem, negotiating the terms he wanted to use, even as his own brothers made jokes about what he was about to attempt.

"Go home and take care of the sheep," they told him.

Instead, he went out before Goliath, picked up five smooth stones just in case one wasn't enough, put one in his slingshot, and let it fly.

David won.

WINNING IS BEING GREATER THAN YOURSELF

Just as winning isn't restricted by your own limitations, your desire to win has to be about something greater than yourself.

Selfish winning is actually losing. It destroys you as a person over time. You need to allow yourself to be a part of something greater than just keeping a win/loss tally sheet to brag about.

It's one of the reasons I love being a defense lawyer. I have amazing opportunities to make a difference in people's lives, just like the butane honey oil case that produced videos to save other people from a terrible fate.

The key to making sure that winning isn't a selfish pursuit is to define what success looks like.

In my job and life, I try to live by a set of values and priorities because they are not only what gives meaning and purpose to life, but also what guides me through. As an attorney, I try to seek justice, love mercy, and walk humbly. Finding a motto to live by helps define what winning is and what you want to achieve in life. It provides meaning, purpose, and direction. And, based on my own life experiences, the less selfish that motto is, the more fulfilling your life will be.

SEEK JUSTICE

In everything I do, I have to ask myself, "Is this just?" Justice says the punishment must fit the crime. Someone who accidentally spills water on your laptop is different from someone who purposefully pours water on it. Even though the end result is the same for you, the punishment should be different.

As a prosecutor in California, I represented the people of the state. But who is a part of that group? The person I'm prosecuting is part of the people, too. What is just and fair for them must also be considered. As a defense attorney, my job is to protect my clients from being the victims of injustice.

> **AS AN ATTORNEY, I TRY TO SEEK JUSTICE, LOVE MERCY, AND WALK HUMBLY.**

LOVE MERCY

Don't people deserve a second chance? Showing mercy and letting someone's story be heard doesn't mean they take no responsibility. It's easy to get a hardened heart and start seeing people as cases to file instead of as human beings with lives, but there should be interplay between justice and mercy.

In *The Merchant of Venice*, we get a picture of mercy in Portia's famous speech to Shylock. Portia is disguised as a lawyer, pleading for mercy for Antonio. Shakespeare wisely noted that mercy must flavor justice. It has to be a part of it, or there is no justice.

WALK HUMBLY

It's easy to have a giant ego as a lawyer because the nature of holding someone's future in your hands feeds the ego. Lawyers went to law school.

WINNING IS NOT, AND CANNOT BE, ABOUT VENGEANCE.

They're trained to win arguments and have used that ability in and out of the courtroom. They've bested other people for a living.

I have to always be checking myself and valuing other people as much as myself, no matter whether they are the judge, the court reporter, support staff, or a client. I try to find ways to justly resolve cases that respect people's time, won't break up families, and in general, keep the human element in the forefront.

If I get these three right, losing doesn't affect me in the same way as someone fixated on winning purely for sport. A loss means I have a chance to learn and a chance to see how something fits into the larger scheme of things. That larger scheme can seem like a puzzle, but the key to solving it is my faith. It's because of my faith that I take defending people seriously and have faith that things will always work out in the end.

Keeping my faith in mind when I'm working a case keeps me from slipping into a place where I take pleasure in someone else's punishment.

If the goal is justice, it can't also be revenge.

Unfortunately, the criminal justice system seems to thrive more on vengeance than rehabilitation. It's not built to want the best for someone, but instead, it's mostly concerned on doling out punishment. It's no surprise why winning can become twisted in such a system, where winning at any cost might make sense.

Winning is not, and cannot be, about vengeance.

No justice system can be just if it is a tool for vengeance. Such a system is an *injustice* system that destroys society by pitting people against each other.

A lack of emphasis on crime prevention has led to a justice system that is reactive instead of proactive. It's only capable of punishing past conduct rather than finding ways to fix the problem, constantly slapping patches on society's leaking pipes. Making those butane honey oil videos didn't bring me fame and glory, and it didn't dole out punishment, but it did help build a better society.

Think about the extremely common problem of mail theft. It happens all the time and can carry serious penalties. One of the ways to reduce this problem is to remove the opportunity by using central locked mailbox systems. This is what crime prevention looks like. It spots recurring problems and looks for solutions instead of new punishments. Crime prevention is like preemptive mercy.

For people who equate justice with punishment, this might seem frustrating. Why change how we set up mailboxes just because some people can't keep their hands off of other people's property? Well, we can fix the mailboxes, or we can keep spending money and time investigating, arresting, trying, and locking people up. More crime equals bigger government.

Ultimately, the question is whether you just want to punish the bad guys or if you want to make a difference in people's lives so they have an opportunity to change. Does winning look like people locked away or people being changed?

A COMPLETE PICTURE OF WINNING

A half-finished painting isn't much to look at, and an incomplete picture of what winning looks like is just as ugly.

You must start by defining what it means to win and what it means to lose. If you're on a winning streak, don't let that feed your ego and make you overconfident. Not only does that create arrogant people, but it also sets you up to lose because you get sloppy with preparation and critical thinking.

On the flip side, don't lose confidence because of your losses.

Of more importance is the manner in which you win or lose. That's as important as anything. If you win, be humble. If you lose, don't blame others. Be gracious instead, accepting responsibility, because that's part of learning, and that's your pathway to the next win.

Winning isn't everything. It isn't even the only thing. There are more important, life-changing concerns—for yourself and for others—at stake.

CLOSING REMARKS

A win or a loss is possible in every situation.

There's no sure thing because human factors can't be controlled or predicted. You can play the best game possible and still lose.

When you win, learn from your opponent's loss.

It's in the loss that the learning resides because it's an opportunity to learn from mistakes. Over time, as you gain experience, you build up your intuition. You get a better sense of situations and people. You're able to pick up on situational shifts that require a change in tactics. Human factors become more understandable.

Winning at any cost is always a failure because not only can it lead to ethical compromise, but you deprive yourself of the hidden benefits that come from a loss.

Success isn't always winning, because success isn't selfish. It seeks justice and good for a greater purpose.

CONCLUSION

In life, you'll have many trials.

That's why the information in this book applies to everyone. Whether it's an external or internal battle, you are always somewhere in the processes I've described in this book. What I've learned as a trial attorney can be put into practice in nearly every situation you face because most of our interactions with people are some form of negotiation, some phase of a courtroom trial. The methodology outlined in these chapters is universal.

This book has shown you how to identify what you can control, how to manage it, and how to use it. It starts with knowing what you want and building the best foundation to get there. Then, through evaluation and critical thinking, you know what you need to do to prepare. Understanding the dynamics and context of a situation helps you know where you stand when it comes time to package everything up for persuasion and negotiation.

Skills for persuasion and negotiation are in high demand. Whether online or in person, at work or simply trying to choose a place to eat—nearly everything we do involves some form of persuasion or negotiation.

Of course, it's inevitable that somewhere in the process, something will go sideways. Unpredictability is about the only thing you can predict.

So, while you can't control everything, the methods in this book show you that you can control many things. You can control what matters in getting you to your destination. You might not be able to control the water, but you can control the rudder on your boat and use that water to get where you want to go.

Ultimately, it all comes down to understanding winning and losing, and your definition of what those are will define how you experience life. I hope I've shown you that dedication to the entire process is how you win, whether or not the verdict comes in as you want. I have faith that things will always work out in the end.

Deep down, everyone wants a protector, a defender in times of trouble. When a child has a nightmare, they call out to their parents. When someone finds themselves dragged into court, they call out to an attorney. When people's lives become filled with problems bigger than they can handle, they call on God.

Even if things don't turn out exactly the way you planned, there is always a reason, always a lesson.

Every step you take is one that you've thought about. That's a win.

Every decision you make is one you've prepared for. That's a win.

Every interaction causes you to think and reconsider. That's a win.

Every situation reveals your strengths but also where you need to grow. That's a win.

Every negotiation teaches you more about how to understand people. That's a win.

Each opportunity to control your emotion and use your mind is a win. You don't get lucky. You don't accidentally succeed. You don't need to view every situation as a gamble. You don't see winning as something that is so narrow that victory is mostly defined by who you've defeated instead of how you've grown. Justice should always take mercy into account. We view being merciful as crucial to winning. You don't see winning as all or nothing, but instead, reap the benefits of how shades of winning and losing enrich your life.

Whether you're in the courtroom, the meeting room, or at the car dealership, what you've learned in this book will help you find meaningful success every single time. When the time comes, you're ready to make your case in the courtroom and wherever else you find yourself in life.

ACKNOWLEDGEMENTS

I would like to acknowledge the following people for the roles they've played in getting me to where I am today:

My Wife: You are the person most responsible for getting me to where I am today. You made it possible for me to make the jump from a steady paycheck to starting my own business. You have taught me the importance of people, of empathy, of listening, and of looking at things from a different perspective. You motivate me to always want to succeed. You help me keep my priorities straight. Thank you from the bottom of my heart for all that you've done and all that you continue to do. I love you.

My Parents: Your love and support made so many things possible for me in life. Without you and the sacrifices you made for my benefit, I would not be where I am today. Thank you for always encouraging me, for stressing the importance of education when I was younger, for getting me through college, and for giving me a roof over my head while I was still in law school. Thank you for your continued support of my career, and for taking such an active role in childcare so that I can continue to advance in my career. I love you both.

My Grandparents: Thank you for your love and your financial support that helped me through college and law school. When I said I was going to go to law school, I remember how proud you all were, and since then, I've always tried to continue making you proud in all that I do and accomplish.

My Siblings: Thanks for putting up with me as we were growing up and as I went through law school. I'm proud of both of you, your accomplishments, and your amazing families. Thank you for always being excited for me, whether it's baking me a cake to celebrate success in my business or flying a flag over the capital when I was taking the bar exam. I love you.

My In-Laws: You have been like a second set of parents to me, and for that I am thankful. Your help with childcare has also made my career pursuits possible. I could not have gotten where I am today without your love and support. I know I can always rely on you through the tough times. Also, thank you to my brother-in-law and his wife; you are definitely an example of a power couple, and you were so supportive when I started my business. I love you all and the love you give to my family.

Coco: You've taught me important things about life. Above all, you've reinforced just how important family is by your selfless dedication to your own family. You have also shown me the importance of letting loose and having fun. You taught me that it's OK not to be serious all the time, and you've given me good advice about business. When I first began talking about starting my own business, you were one of the loudest voices encouraging me to do it. Thank you to your family, who has embraced me as family, too. I love you all! Muchas gracias por todo.

Jamil Frazier: Thank you for taking the time to talk with me when I first began my business. Without your guidance, I would have never even considered writing a book, nor would I have known anything about Jordan or Story Chorus.

Jordan Loftis, Mark Henderson, Anna Thompson, and all of the wonderful people at Story Chorus: It has been a pleasure working with you to bring this book to life. Your expertise has made this process smooth and enjoyable. I'm excited about what doors are being opened and for the future projects I'm sure we'll be collaborating on soon.

Alan Tate: You played a pivotal role in my legal career. You were my first supervisor when I was clerking at the DA's office, and if not for you, your guidance, mentorship, and friendship, I have no doubt that my career path would have been very different. You deserve a big part of the credit for my decade-long career at the Riverside County District Attorney's Office and for the successful career I enjoyed as a prosecutor. Thank you.

Tim Hollenhorst: You were one of my best mentors at the DA's office, and I'm glad to still call you a friend. You helped me better understand what it means to pursue justice. You were also the person who started me on my eventual transition from prosecutor to defense attorney, though at the time I didn't know it. Your willingness to leave your career behind as a successful prosecutor in the pursuit of justice inspired me to eventually do the same, just in a different way.

ABOUT THE AUTHOR

Greg Rollins has practiced criminal law as an attorney in California since passing the nation's hardest bar exam in 2010. Greg worked for nearly a decade as a prosecutor with the Riverside County District Attorney's Office, and he won several awards for outstanding trial work, including the Riverside County Misdemeanor Prosecutor of the Year two years in a row. Greg also played an integral role in creating the Riverside County District Attorney's Office's award-winning butane honey oil awareness videos in 2018.

After a prestigious career as a prosecutor, Greg began a new chapter in his legal career by opening his own criminal defense law practice, The Law

Office of Gregory Rollins. He has also been recognized as a member of the 2020 National Trial Lawyers Top 100 and as a 2020 National Academy of Criminal Defense Lawyers Top 10 Under 40. He is currently a member of the Christian Legal Society, the National Trial Lawyers, and the National Academy of Criminal Defense Lawyers.

In his free time, Greg enjoys spending time with his family, visiting Disneyland, and playing board games. He is widely respected in the Riverside legal community, with a reputation for seeking justice and being committed to excellence.

Made in the USA
Monee, IL
17 March 2022

f864dd14-dc3f-4e33-8ae5-6291c1cfdb5eR01